LAST TRACES:
THE LOST ART OF AUSCHWITZ

LAST TRACES

THE LOST ART OF AUSCHWITZ

Photography and Text by JOSEPH P. CZARNECKI

Introduction by CHAIM POTOK

ATHENEUM   *New York   1989*

Atheneum
Macmillan Publishing Company
866 Third Avenue, New York, N.Y. 10022
Collier Macmillan Canada, Inc.

Library of Congress Cataloging-in-Publication Data
Czarnecki, Joseph P.
    Last traces : the lost art of Auschwitz / photography and text by
Joseph P. Czarnecki.
       p.   cm.
    ISBN 0-689-12022-2
    1. Mural painting and decoration—20th century—Poland—Oświęcim.
2. Auschwitz (Poland : concentration camp) in art.   3. Holocaust,
Jewish (1939–1945), in art.   I. Title.
ND2812.P620834   1989
751.7′3′094385—dc19   88-38496   CIP

Macmillan books are available at special discounts for bulk
purchases for sales promotions, premiums, fund-raising, or
educational use. For details, contact:
   Special Sales Director
   Macmillan Publishing Company
   866 Third Avenue
   New York, N.Y. 10022

Design by Janet Tingey

10 9 8 7 6 5 4 3 2 1

Printed in the United States of America

To my dear wife Grażyna

CONTENTS

ACKNOWLEDGMENTS

I would first like to thank Kazimierz Smolen and the entire staff of the State Museum at Oswiecim (Auschwitz), without whose unstinting assistance this book would never have been possible. Special credit must go to Auschwitz historian Adam Cyra, who shared his intimate knowledge of Auschwitz history with me, and also to historians Jerzy Debski and Franciszek Piper. Lydia Foryciarz made the museum's darkroom available to me, and, with Stanislaw Mucha, was responsible for much of the original documentation of the paintings and inscriptions found in this book.

It was Dr. Tadeusz Kinowski, the art conservation director of the museum (now retired), who first brought the existence of many of the works in this book to my attention and made it possible for me to photograph them. His successor, Witold Smrek, was invaluable in organizing carpenters and electricians on parts of the project that required scaffolding to be built or electricity to be brought into unused spaces. To the museum staff, from the guards who stood by to open and close doors during nighttime shoots, to the librarians who helped me wend my way through the maze of camp registers, I express my sincerest thanks.

I owe special debts of gratitude to Cornell Capa of the International Center of Photography, who came through with a generous grant of money and materials at a crucial point in this project; to *New York Times* Warsaw correspondent Michael Kaufman, whose early encouragement provided a much needed boost for the project; and to Mike's father for his careful reading of the text and for sharing his knowledge of Jakub Kozielczuk.

I would like to thank Lucjan Motyka, Jan Pilecki, Zofia Zdrowak, Tadeusz Pietrzykowski and Mieczyslaw Koscielniak for taking the time to recall some very painful memories of their experiences in Auschwitz. All of them have added immensely to the value of this book.

I would like to thank my assistant, Arthur Pawlikowski, for his stamina, ingenuity and patience, the people at the Foton film factory in Warsaw, for cutting my sheet film, and the director of Golleschau cement works for giving me access to the murals there. Thanks also to Witek Krassowski for allowing me to use his darkroom.

Finally, I would like to thank my wife and family for their support and patience in tolerating my long absences from home.

JOSEPH CZARNECKI
Warsaw, May 1, 1988

x

INTRODUCTION

Each time we think the frightful landscape of the Holocaust no longer has anything to offer us for further exploration—the death events by now a predictable litany: roundup, deportation, cattle car, arrival, selection, gas chamber, crematorium; and the survivors' tales a recurrent threnody: work camp, slave labor, degradation, starvation, cunning, blind luck, liberation—we turn a corner and come upon hitherto unexplored and startling terrain. It is quite as if that world of darkness, having once been opened to us, continues to be present, relentlessly, infinitely, as we find ourselves stumbling again and again upon new aspects of its demonic and transfixing topography.

Much valuable work has been done in recent years unearthing, evaluating, and presenting the art produced in concentration camps and ghettos during the period of the Second World War. I have in mind exhibits of this art that I have seen during the past decade and a half and the books I have read that deal with it, among them the notable volume by Mary S. Costanza, *The Living Witness.*

In a concentration camp a specialized skill could save one's life or postpone one's death. Those who possessed such skills—physicians, architects, engineers, mechanics, tailors, musicians, dentists, barbers, carpenters, shoemakers, artists—were put into the service of the Nazis. Simon Wiesenthal, the man who has dedicated his life to unearthing Nazi killers, was spared because of his artistic abilities. In a forced-labor camp he painted swastikas and eagle shields on captured Russian locomotives. He became a sign painter and then worked as a draftsman and architect. One day his name appeared on the execution list. He stood naked on the edge of a pit, waiting to be shot, when he heard his name called. He was returned to headquarters and ordered to make signs and a huge poster to celebrate Hitler's fifty-fourth birthday.

Ms. Costanza tells us that there were studios and workshops in some of the camps where artists "were permitted to do their own work, if it was not offensive to the authorities, after the fulfillment of their prison assignments." Many of those artists, at great risk to themselves, engaged in clandestine art and created a record in images of the world into which they had been plunged. What they feared more than death was the possibility that the hellish nightmare in which they now lived and would most likely die would simply wink out and never be known. They drew and painted the nightmare, concealed their work in various places—barracks walls, the earth, bunks, lofts—or managed to get it smuggled out of the camps, hoping that the future would somehow stumble across it.

Joseph P. Czarnecki stumbled across some of the art contained between the covers of this book—in a latrine.

Nearly two million people were murdered in Auschwitz between May 1940 and January 1945. Ninety percent were Jews. It is much to the credit of Mr. Czarnecki that he recognizes the chilling incongruity between today's Auschwitz, with its "innocuous-looking buildings laid out in neat rows across tree-lined avenues" and the vision of the man-made inferno that the very name "Auschwitz" immediately thrusts before our eyes. But the real Auschwitz, that vast effluvium emanating from humankind's proclivity for evil, still exists—if one knows where to seek it out.

As a photojournalist, Mr. Czarnecki often covered the visits of dignitaries to the Auschwitz museum. Time and repetition normally dull even the most sensitive of hearts, yet Mr. Czarnecki began to notice things previously ignored by him and others: drawings in latrines and washrooms; murals in the children's barracks; here and there strange scratchings, paintings, inscriptions, decorations—all on the walls of Auschwitz.

An inquiry addressed to the art conservation director of the museum brought an astonishing response: There exists an inventory on cards of almost all that can be seen on the walls of that silenced inferno. Aided by the staff of the museum, Mr. Czarnecki began the painstaking task of searching for and photographing this art. Much of it was in basements and attics long closed to the public. The result is this quite remarkable book. Its purpose is, in the words of the author, "to show the victims' attempts to express themselves in some way." As such, it often brings tears to the eyes and rage to the heart.

The walls of Auschwitz—witnesses to this century's worst horrors—contain many different kinds of art: paintings, drawings, scratchings. A mural depicts the killing work done by those in the penal company; another, found in the subcamp at Golleschau, enables us to view prisoners in a rock quarry. There are latrine and washroom decorations, and slogans urging the inmates to guard against typhus and extolling the virtues of cleanliness and personal hygiene. Here and there shafts of grim humor work their way through the darkness: a painting of a distraught and quite possibly drunk apothecary; another of a mocking chimney sweep; caricatures in an out-of-the-way storage attic of Hitler and Mussolini. Much of the art was commissioned by prisoners acting in a supervisory capacity and eager to please their Nazi overlords. Virtually all the paintings are by hands now unknown. Most of the art is crude, amateurish, functional.

And yet—and yet—we gaze upon the walls that bear the art, and the art enters a dimension of meaning we do not normally attribute to the ordinary doodle, the ever-present, quickly scanned and forgotten poster, the "Kilroy was here" scratching, the graffiti that blight the surfaces of the contemporary world. The art of Auschwitz is encased in a membrane of experience so unique that it forces a reevaluation of all notions of good and bad art. We do not gaze upon the art on those walls in terms of the aesthetics of form, line, color, planar arrangement. Like the art of the cave dwellers, this art is a record of events in a certain slice of human existence. It is art washed by a special circumstance that renders it all equally valuable, equally compelling, equally unique. Normal aesthetic criteria are here put aside. Art born in Auschwitz makes its own criteria.

Think, if you will, of the hands that painted the mysterious ballerina, the rabbit, the nudes. Think of the weary body that carved the Sacred Heart figure into a plaster wall. Think of the fingers that drew the hearts of lovers and scratched and carved names and numbers and final words on the walls and doors and bricks of the Death Block. Conjure up the hearts and minds of the Jews, Poles, Russians, Germans, Dutch, Hungarians, Yugoslavians, Greeks, French, and Italians who created the art in this book. In the world outside Auschwitz, the artist and his efforts count for nothing as we go about evaluating a work of art. Inside Auschwitz the effort is everything, and the record it leaves behind, no matter how crude its form, more than equals that of any past human attempts to document and come to terms with the cataclysms that beset us. The art of Auschwitz is the art of the witness.

Particularly poignant, an apt and ghostly pair of metaphors for that charnel house, are two drawings. One depicts a clock without hands, the other shows us time floating away on a kite. Time is a function of duration marked and segmented by value. Valueless duration is time-less: a world without humanity, dignity, culture, the beats and syncopations that mark and charge the cadenced days of our lives. There was no time as we know it in Auschwitz, only the lurches and shocks of a demonic creation wholly dedicated to slaughter.

Why did they make this art? What is this propensity we have for recording our presence even in the chambers of Hell? "The paintings were the equivalent of what we didn't have," one artist explained to the author after the war. Mr. Czarnecki states that "one of art's basic functions is to be a witness to life, to depict how life was at a specific time and place." Art was not a cultural frivolity to the inmates of Auschwitz; it literally kept their spirits alive. It was self-expression in the teeth of the annihilation of the self. It was an expression of the need to retain psychological coherence in a malevolent ambience whose essential purpose was the destruction of the psyche of its inhabitants. The words "I am" written on a wall are the epitaph of someone about to die. Whoever wrote those words—we see them now. "I am." Those words are the "you" we will remember.

Picasso said that "painting is an instrument of war to be waged against brutality and darkness." The pictures on the walls of Auschwitz are such an instrument: a kind of sacred graffiti of the soul. They are a cry: "Look at us! The hands that created us were here once. We are here now! Find us! Expose us to the light! That will continue the existence of those who created us!"

To those artists this volume says: "We have found you. We are looking at you. You continue to exist—as witnesses to this darkest of human events and to the tenacity of the human spirit."

CHAIM POTOK

LAST TRACES: THE LOST ART OF AUSCHWITZ

The idea of painting or drawing was to leave a trace of yourself behind.
—Jozef Szajna, Auschwitz artist[1]

From May 1940, when the first prisoners were brought to Auschwitz, to January 27, 1945, when the Soviet army liberated the camp, almost two million people, ninety percent of whom were Jews, perished in the systematic extermination of conquered peoples and undesirable races that was the heart of Nazi Germany's plan to create a new order in Europe.[2] The statistics are staggering, incomprehensible.

To go to Auschwitz today is to find oneself faced with the enormous incongruity between the innocuous-looking buildings laid out in neat rows along tree-lined avenues and the images of horror that the name Auschwitz conjures up. The wartime photographs and displays of masses of human hair, shoes, spectacles and toothbrushes testify to the scale of the tragedy without evoking the suffering of the individual.

But there is another kind of evidence here. Hidden behind locked basement and attic doors, carved, painted or drawn on walls and woodwork, there exist, still, the last traces of the people who suffered and died here. For more than forty years these images have gone largely ignored by all but a handful of the State Museum staff. These images, the lost art of Auschwitz, are the subject of this book.

I had been working in Poland as a photojournalist since 1980, covering, among other things, the many official and semiofficial visits of Western dignitaries and notables to the Auschwitz museum. Some came to remember one of the camp's solemn anniversaries; others made it a routine stop on their political pilgrimages to Poland. All these were occasions for taking photographs under the camp gates, with their ironic greeting: ARBEIT MACHT FREI (Work Makes Free).

These routine working visits to Auschwitz had somewhat inured me to the profound feelings of shock, rage, grief and despair that usually overwhelm the first-time visitor; and at last, out of simple curiosity, I began noticing things that I, like so many others, had previously passed by.

My first discoveries were in the dilapidated but still-standing remains of the women's camp in Birkenau, where I came upon several outlying buildings that had been latrines and washrooms. One had a drawing of a toothpaste tube and a shaving brush on the wall; another, a rising sun with the words "Sun, Air, Water" in German. That these images were to be found in a place where hundreds of people were forced to relieve themselves in just a few minutes makes them all the more ironic.

Other images I found during my first explorations include the Königsgraben mural and the two murals in the children's barracks, all in the women's camp in Birkenau and accessible to the tourist willing to look around a bit. On later trips I made an exact inventory of the entire women's camp, and then went to the museum's art conservation director, Dr. Tadeusz Kinowski, to see what he could tell me about the artwork I had located.

Much to my surprise, he showed me a card file, made about twenty years ago, which constituted a fairly complete inventory of what could be seen on the walls of Auschwitz, catalogued block by block. Much of the painting was the simple stenciled or patterned wall decoration one still sees in Eastern European farmhouses, but there were also complete paintings, drawings, initials and inscriptions. Each card gave a brief description, with the creator of the work in the few cases where this was known, and a small identifying photograph.

With the help of the museum staff, I began systematically searching the barracks, floor by floor and inch by inch. There were a few images in rooms open to tourists, but the most interesting ones I found were in basements and attics, many of which had been closed for years. The basement prison cells of Block 11, the notorious Death Block, turned out to be filled with inscriptions, and I am still finding new ones there that I must have overlooked on earlier trips. Some of the images scratched into the cell walls, for example, could be seen only when illuminated from an extremely acute angle, and I missed several such inscriptions even after repeated examinations. Most of my searching was done either with a very strong flashlight or with a thousand-watt halogen light; these allowed me to pick out markings that were very faint or hidden under layers of dust. There is no telling what might be found using more sophisticated methods of examining painted or scratched surfaces.

Most of the images catalogued in the card file were still in place, but a few had already fallen to the ravages of time. Anything done on a plaster surface, especially in a basement or attic, was particularly vulnerable, which is why several of the smaller items photographed twenty years ago have since disappeared. And, though it appears that the museum's founders took care to paint around the images they found, some may have been painted over in the postwar years when many of the barracks were renovated and made into exhibition areas. Especially susceptible to this were the small inscriptions and initials, many of which may have been ignored or gone unseen by the workmen. Successive generations have also left their marks on the walls, from the Russian soldiers who liberated the camp, to the German prisoners of war who were kept here for a few months after the war, to tourists of every nationality.

The German prisoners of war left quite a few drawings, which sometimes made the process of distinguishing them from the concentration-camp drawings somewhat complicated. Several cartoonlike drawings in Birkenau turned out to have been made in the summer of 1945, probably by these soldiers. Nearby pictures of a similar graphic character, although undated, were assumed to be from the same period. A large mural of a train entering the camp seemed at first glance to be a straightforward documentation of prisoners entering the camp—except for the fact that the passengers were smiling. The drawing turned out to have been made in July 1945.

In the majority of cases, however, the paintings and drawings I found were located in locked areas and had been more or less forgotten. This made the process of discovery quite exciting.

In the case of a painting of a ballerina (jacket photograph), I doubt that an archaeologist opening up an Egyptian tomb could have felt more anticipation. The painting, whose location had been recorded in the card file, was hidden behind a mound of cement sacks in a basement that had been made into a storage area. A ballerina in Auschwitz! By some standards, I suppose, she is less than perfect—an arm a bit too fat, fingers a bit too long, foot a bit too stubby and colors more than a bit too bright —but there she was, calm and serene as a Buddha in this charnel house.

To find my way to "The Apothecary" I had to climb up to the top of Block 28, which used to be the camp hospital. The painting was done on a sloping plastered ceiling in an attic that was used as a storehouse for medicines and herbs taken from prisoners arriving on the transports. It was propped up by a large piece of plywood held in place by wooden beams wedged into the floor, and several workers had to be engaged to delicately remove this support long enough for a picture to be taken.

While we know "The Apothecary" to be the work of Tadeusz Myszkowski, a well-known camp artist who survived the war and who worked briefly afterward as camp art director before emigrating to Israel, most of the paintings that appear in this book are unattributed. In a few instances there is a name or prisoner number that identifies the artist. I was able to track down only one of these, Lucjan Motyka, who made three paintings on the wall of a washroom in Block 8 during one week in August 1943. What he told me sheds much light on how many of the other paintings probably came to be created:

"I came to Auschwitz relatively late, in 1943, because I had spent almost a year in prison in Krakow, where I was tortured. I tried to hang myself so that I wouldn't betray my friends, but the belt broke. After that a guard kind of looked after me so that I survived and was sent to Auschwitz. Block 8 was the so-called quarantine block, where arriving prisoners were kept temporarily before being assigned to the kommandos, or work details, some to digging sand, others to factories. This was very heavy work, and, practically speaking, assignment to one of these details meant death in a few months' time.

"When I was brought to the block, the capo [an overseer of a work detail] asked if anybody knew how to paint. The Germans had created a kind of competition between blocks, and had the prisoners do the halls and stairways to look like marble. Since we in quarantine had not yet been assigned to work details, this was the time they had us do the painting.

"I had done some painting before the war in a workers' club—decoration and that sort of thing. I didn't know much about technique, such as mixing paint, but I had a talent for drawing and making portraits and posters. So when the capo asked who could paint, I spoke out, because everybody was looking for some possibility, some way to get out of the work details. Besides, I had arrived at Auschwitz in an undernourished condition, and I thought it would be good to latch onto that kind of work. One had to respect work like that. I took as long as I could, about seven days, to complete the three paintings.

"Our capo was a German-speaking Pole from Silesia named

Bednarek. He wanted someone to paint the bathroom, a landscape or something like that. I was not really the initiator of the contents of the paintings—he was. He gave me water-based chalk paints, the kind that are used to paint houses, and with these I created two landscapes and a bathroom mirror. The capo told me to paint the room so that it looked orderly; and I knew that the Germans were fond of the kind of slogans that hang on kitchen walls, so I added the words *Sauberkeit ist Gesundheit* [Cleanliness is Health] to the bottom of the mirror painting. The capo was satisfied, because there was this competition to show the Germans they knew how to keep order. These were not, of course, works of art, but given the conditions, circumstances provided the inspiration.

"The paintings were the equivalent of what we didn't have. A man in prison thinks of mountains and space, so I painted a mountain landscape. Everyone thought of space. There was also a certain element of irony. The prisoners used to laugh: 'My, don't we have an elegant bathroom!' Really, all our efforts were directed at keeping people together psychologically."

This is probably how many of the wall paintings originated. A capo, trying to impress his German masters with his love of order and cleanliness, enlisted whatever talent fell within his jurisdiction. In turn, the practice became so popular that it fostered a certain amount of competition between blocks.

Despite the fact that many of these works were "commissioned," and thus represent the tastes of the jailers (a kind of middle-class German kitsch), it would be a mistake to assume that they do were devoid of self-expression. Motyka's bathroom-mirror painting, for example, is a good piece of creative draughtsmanship that also expressed the artist's sense of irony and, in this macabre environment, served a life-enhancing purpose by lifting the inmates' spirits with a moment's humor.

There was also a more organized aspect to art at Auschwitz. In the fall of 1941, at the suggestion of a Polish artist, Franciszek Targosz, camp commandant Rudolf Hoss ordered a museum to be established, with Targosz as the capo in charge. One of the first tasks of the artists was to create a pseudo-documentation that would demonstrate the racial inferiority of gypsies and Jews and other groups incarcerated in the camp; but their work was soon expanded to include the informal production of portraits, greeting cards, cigarette cases and all sorts of small sculpted pieces, which were used as a form of exchange with the SS men.

Along with this commissioned work, many of the artists produced clandestine drawings demonstrating the horrible conditions that existed in the camp, some of which were smuggled out at great risk. The "museum" also saved lives by providing alternative work for many artists, who were thus able to avoid the deadly work details. Targosz is credited with having saved a number of lives by finding men places in the museum workshop.[3]

There is at least some overlap between the artists who created the wall paintings and those who worked in the museum. Tadeusz Myszkowski was a camp-museum artist, but Lucjan Motyka was not. In most cases, the lack of attribution makes it impossible to differentiate between the work of the museum painters and the work of others.

The clear division that does occur in this book is between the commissioned art (however much self-expression may or may not be present) and the spontaneous art, which was executed freely (clandestinely). Also, with just a few exceptions, I have chosen not to include an entire category of images found in many places on the walls of Auschwitz—the numerous slogans enjoining adherence to health regulations and warning signs of various sorts. Many of these are painted very exactly, often in elegant Gothic script, and are quite interesting in certain respects. Nevertheless, their inclusion would interfere with the main purpose of this book, which is to show the victims' attempts to express themselves in some way.

A problem of dating the inscriptions sometimes arose in connection with the cells of Block 11, which were occupied not only by concentration-camp prisoners, but also later by German prisoners of war. The tourists, especially those who came immediately after the war, left their marks as well. Tourist markings, fortunately, are generally broad, rambling and careless, usually a name, date and hometown.

The prisoners' markings, on the other hand, are almost always carefully done and are usually quite small. This is undoubtedly due to the fact that the inmates had much time but little material, perhaps nothing more than an inch-long piece of pencil lead that someone had managed to smuggle in.

Undated German-language inscriptions in these cells are difficult to evaluate and have therefore been excluded, as have several calendars and dated inscriptions obviously the work of German prisoners of war.

One basement was filled with images that were quite simply pornographic—the sort of thing one might find in public toilets. The likelihood of this being tolerated by the Germans seemed so slight that the more probable explanation is that it was done by German soldiers after the war, or possibly by the SS men. A nude I found on the wall of a room where Germans performed gynecological experiments on women was also of questionable origin. Despite the barbarity of the Nazi enterprise, there was a kind of bourgeois order about it that would probably not have allowed such a frivolous expression of sexuality. These, and others that I could not be certain were from the occupation period, I have decided to omit rather than risk compromising the validity or authenticity of the victims' work.

Most of the images collected here come from Auschwitz I, the main camp, rather than from Auschwitz II, or Birkenau, because the wooden barracks of Birkenau were almost all dismantled immediately after the war. The only barracks that survived in Birkenau were the brick structures in the women's camp. I have included one of the surviving four murals from the subcamp at Golleschau (now Goleszow), which was part of what was called "Auschwitz III," but have otherwise not explored any of the surviving subcamp structures. As far as I know, these other buildings do not contain any significant artwork, although it may still be possible to find scattered inscriptions here and there.

It should also be made clear that the art of Auschwitz was made by prisoners from the numbered and registered group of more than 405,000 who were either "selected" for work out of the transports or brought to Auschwitz for political or other reasons. The massive transports of Jews brought to Auschwitz for extermination did not, for the most part, even enter the camp. These people went straight to the gas chambers, or else were held in the camp for only a brief period; in either case, they were not entered in the camp records. The artwork that was done in one of these temporary camps, the Theresienstadt family camp, has, unfortunately, not survived.

Out of the hundreds of signatures and often only partly legible inscriptions found on window frames, doors, pillars, beams, cell doors and walls, I have, of necessity, had to choose only a handful of representative ones for this book. Nevertheless, in bypassing every brick or inscription where a name was faintly or only partially visible, and therefore less "photogenic," I felt the burden of having the few images that were visible speak for the vast majority of the silent dead.

The chapter organization and categorization of the images that follow reflect my view that these traces are part of a philosophical process of affirmation. Despite the degradation and dehumanization that the camps imposed, the process of making art still functioned in a vital way as a means of recovering and reclaiming the rites of life and of death. It is to this indomitable life force that I bow my head in making this book.

POEM ON LINTEL OF CELL DOOR

The walls of Auschwitz are covered with markings that time has rendered illegible—fragments of signatures, pieces of poems, names and addresses. I had bypassed this particular inscription several times, since I had been told that several experts had been unable to make any sense of it. On one of my last trips to Auschwitz I decided to photograph it, on the chance that I might be able to find an expert in the Old Gothic script in which it was written. This expert I found in the person of Renata Marsch, the Warsaw correspondent for DPA, the German press agency. She was able to decipher almost all of the text and translate the inscription into modern German.[4] The subsequent translation from German into English was made by my father, Joseph L. Czarnecki, and my sister-in-law, Heidi Czarnecki.

The use of the Old Gothic script suggests that the author was an educated German or Austrian about forty or fifty years old, since in Hitler's time the modern alphabet was already in widespread use. The wording suggests that the man was of a religious nature, possibly even a clergyman or priest.

Man draws his lot at birth
And must travel the way predestined
    for him
Whether he wants to or not.

Fate is without feeling or love,
And asks no one whether it is right for
    him.

Thus runs the path into the
    unknown,
Straight and winding,
Uphill and downhill,
Narrow and wide.

Some stumble and fall, rise again,
And shake off the dust.
The wounds heal quickly,
And all is well again.

A beautiful goal beckons to many,
Where the sun shines and good
    fortune waits.

A great distant light illuminates
    their way,
That they may proceed more safely.

Then there are streets that lead into
    darkness,
And further into the abyss
Where danger and death lurk.

For those who find themselves
    there,
The sun goes out.

Grace is certainly there,
But is hard to see and comprehend
For those who must wander in the
    darkness.

Poem on Lintel of Cell Door   Block 11, Cell 1
Auschwitz Main Camp   H: 10 inches   W: 4 inches

BEARING WITNESS

One of art's basic functions is to be a witness to life, to depict how life was at a specific time and place. Many concentration-camp artists took great risks in documenting life in the camp and smuggling out these drawings and paintings. Others drew on their experiences and memories to portray these events after the war.

The Königsgraben mural which opens this chapter is all the more remarkable because it was done openly, at the time of the events it depicts. This suggests that the Nazis were arrogant enough, at the time, to think that this work would never stand in witness against them.

There is no other artwork on the walls of Auschwitz, or of any other concentration camp, for that matter, which so directly depicts an event in the life of the camp.

THE PENAL COMPANY

The scene represented here is a slice of life from the penal company, the most brutal work detail in Auschwitz. The facts are presented blandly enough, perhaps less expressionistically than in most of the clandestinely made documents; nevertheless, this work shows unambiguously the murderous effects of the work, which caused prisoners to drop from exhaustion. Jozef Kret, a former inmate and member of the penal company, described it succinctly in these words: "Whoever went through it soon was convinced that the concentration camp was only an anteroom to hell. Hell itself, its very bottom, was the penal company."[5]

Despite the fact that the faces of several of the figures in this painting are clearly rendered (and probably represent real people), no one has ever been able to determine who they and the artist were. The group on the left seem to be functionaries of some sort, and the man holding the shovel may be either the artist or a close friend; but it is impossible to be sure.

What is being represented here is quite clear, however. The entire scene is topped by giant blue Gothic letters reading "Königsgraben" (King's Canal), the name of an irrigation ditch that was being dug by members of the penal company to drain the swampy water away from Birkenau. The letters are not visible in this photograph because they are now covered by wooden beams, which prevent the sloped ceiling from collapsing. The picture can still be seen by tourists willing to go slightly out of their way to find Block 1 in Birkenau, but this entire section of ceiling will soon be removed, restored and warehoused, to prevent further damage; it will be replaced by a facsimile.

The penal company was housed in Block 11, the Death Block, in the main camp, and was moved to Birkenau on May 9,

The Penal Company
"Königsgraben"
Birkenau, Block 1
H: 108 inches
W: 150 inches

1942. Sometime between then and July 15, 1943, when Birkenau became a women's camp, this mural was created.

In the beginning, primarily Jews and priests were assigned to the penal company. Later, it became a place of punishment for offenses ranging from escape attempts to contact with civilians to such minor infractions as smoking during work or just moving too slowly for an SS man's taste. Political prisoners were also sent to this company. Sentences ranged from one month to life, but a prolonged stay almost certainly meant death.

Penal-company prisoners got up earlier than other prisoners, worked longer hours and were given less food. Breakfast was black coffee or herb tea, and at noon there was a soup of turnips, potatoes and other vegetables, often rotten. Supper consisted of some bread with tea. As additional punishment, a prisoner might not get even this pittance for two or three days. Prisoners could not send or receive mail, were not allowed to smoke and only in rare instances were treated in the prison hospital.

Worst of all were the beatings that constantly accompanied all work. One of the most feared figures in all of Auschwitz was Hauptscharführer Otto Moll, whose very appearance terrified prisoners. Under him was a gang of overseers, or functionaries (drawn from the ranks of criminal prisoners), ready to carry out his sadistic commands. Other SS men made a game out of "hunting" prisoners. A prisoner would be told to get up and run and would then be shot at for target practice until he was killed. The Jews, especially, were favorite victims of this kind of "sport."

It was no wonder, then, that the situation led to escape attempts and even open rebellion. On June 10, 1942, a group of political prisoners facing imminent death in Block 11 decided to make a group escape. The plan was to go into action at the sound of the whistle marking the end of the day's work. Due to a sudden downpour, though, work stopped early. The momentary confusion

*The Penal
Company
"Königsgraben"
Birkenau,
Block 1
Detail 1*

was enough to make some of the would-be escapees hesitate, giving the SS men time to react. Only nine escaped, and thirteen were shot in the attempt; the rest were taken back to the camp. Three were beaten to death on the way by angry SS men. When the prisoners refused to answer questions about the escape attempt, twenty more were shot and the remaining 320 were sent to the gas chamber.[6]

The Penal Company
"Königsgraben"
Birkenau, Block 1
Detail 2

WORK MURALS AT THE GOLLESCHAU SUBCAMP

By 1944, more than 41,000 prisoners were employed in subcamps throughout Silesia. The subcamp at Golleschau, where this mural was found, employed prisoners to manufacture cement and to mine the raw materials necessary for its production.

The mural shown here is one of four that survived (out of six) which depict various aspects of the work. Unlike the Königsgraben mural, these do not give much idea of the murderous conditions under which this work was carried out. Only the shaved heads and striped pants of the prisoners indicate that this was forced labor.

Prisoners at Work
in Rock Quarry
Golleschau Subcamp
H: 78 inches
W: 120 inches

MAN BEING SHAVED

The attic where these drawings were found may have served as the block barbershop. Each block had its own barber, and prisoners had to be shaved twice a week. This was done by the barber, of course, since prisoners were not allowed to have razors.

Man Being Shaved
(left side of pair)
Block 14, attic
Main Camp
H: 14 inches

Man Being Shaved
(right side of pair)
Block 14, attic
Main Camp
H: 14 inches

ART TO ORDER

Much of the larger-scale art at Auschwitz was "commissioned" by functionaries trying to please their German masters. Functionaries were prisoners who worked in a supervisory capacity either in the blocks or on work details (where they were called "capos"). The first functionaries were German criminals (called "greens," which referred to the color of the identifying triangle they wore), whose brutality often exceeded that of the SS men. As time went on, more and more of these positions were taken over by political prisoners ("reds"), as the camp's resistance movement worked to get more of its own people into positions of authority. But even among the thirty original functionaries, there were a few, prisoners recall, who behaved relatively decently; so the designation "functionary" should not necessarily be taken to mean a brutal criminal overseer, although many of them would have fit this description quite well.

Decorating the washrooms and latrines seems to have been one of the capos' favorite projects. Images of cherubs splashing each other with water and young men riding horses in a pond immediately suggest the Nazi obsession with youth and cleanliness —but, perhaps, with more sinister undertones.

Slogans enjoining cleanliness take on absurd proportions when written in latrines designed for a hundred people at a time. The words "Sun, Air, Water" in such a place might be cruel rather than ironic were it not for the fact that the prisoners probably did not have enough time to notice them.

THE FUNCTIONARIES

The well-fitted, clean uniforms and shiny black shoes identify these three men as functionaries, also called "prominents." Two of the numbers on the chests are readable, and make it possible to determine (from records in the museum archives) that the man on the right arrived on December 13, 1940, from Dachau, while the man in the center arrived in the spring of 1943.[7] This indicates that the painting was probably made around mid-1943, since what seems to be represented here is a kind of welcoming.

Being a functionary meant having certain privileges, and therefore a better opportunity for survival; by the middle of 1943 these privileges included wearing normal everyday shoes instead of the wooden prisoner clogs. It was not uncommon to see functionaries walking about in well-pressed uniforms with polished black shoes that had been "organized" from the Effektenlager (called "Canada"), where property stolen from the arriving Jews was kept. This was a time when watches and diamonds were the currency used to buy bread,[8] and functionaries could use food to buy whatever they wanted from the Canada storehouses.

As Lucjan Motyka described it, it was the functionaries who organized the decoration of many of the blocks, and therefore were responsible for instigating much of the art at Auschwitz.

This painting can be seen by visitors in the stairwell at the back of Block 13, where the Danish and East German exhibits are housed.

*The Functionaries
Block 13,
stairwell
Main Camp
H: 40 inches*

LATRINE AND WASHROOM
WITH SLOGANS

The Nazis seem to have had a penchant for slogans extolling the virtues of cleanliness and health, and the most likely place for them to appear, of course, was in the camp latrines and washrooms. (I photographed just a few of the many I found, because a complete documentation of this aspect of camp art would have taken up a disproportionately large amount of space in this book.) Auschwitz historian Jerzy Debski[9] has studied these slogans in some detail, both those that were painted on moveable signs and those that were painted directly on the walls.

The photograph of the latrine in Birkenau, where hundreds had to relieve themselves in the space of a few minutes, shows how absurd these slogans were. The scenes that occurred in latrines like this one are described in the testimony of survivor Maria Slisz:

"For the care of our physiological needs in Lager Bla there were two brick barracks, latrines, which were always full. In 1943 and '44 there was a cemented-over pit the length of the entire barracks. On both sides of this pit the prisoners crouched on a small cemented rise.

"During the morning the use of the latrine was accompanied by beatings, cries and swearing. The women did not have the strength to push inside the barracks and squatted around the outside, relieving themselves under the open sky, not caring that the guards in the tower were watching. Sometimes for fun they would shoot at us. After a few days there was a stinking pile of human feces in a ring several meters around the barracks. The women, in a rush, slid and fell into this mess, and on more than one occasion did not have the strength to get up and died there."[10]

The latrines pictured are located past the barracks, near the barbed-wire fence, and can be seen by visitors.

Latrine with Slogan
"Cleanliness, Health"
Birkenau
H: 36 inches
W: 62 inches

Washroom with Slogan
"Sun, Air, Water"
Birkenau
H: 36 inches
W: 62 inches

SIMULATED BATHROOM MIRRORS

Washroom Painting
Simulating Bathroom
Mirror
Birkenau
H: 40 inches
W: 62 inches

Although one of these paintings was found in the main camp and the other in Birkenau, they are remarkably similar. Whether the same artist did both or one simply copied the other was impossible to determine.

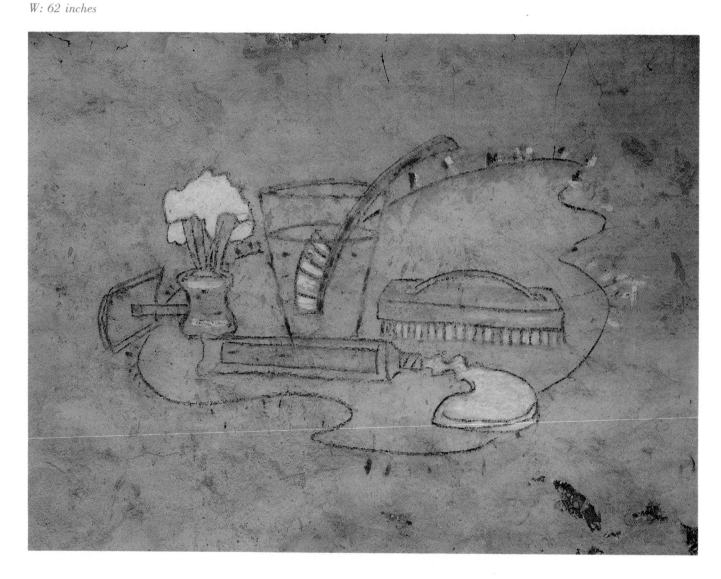

*Washroom Painting
Simulating Bathroom
Mirror
Block 14, ground floor
Main Camp
H: 31 inches
W: 46 inches*

31

HORSEBACK RIDERS, CHERUBS BATHING AND KITTENS

These three paintings are done in rust-colored paint, very likely by the same person, since they are located in the same washroom. In another context they might seem innocent enough, but here they seem to have sinister undertones (the painting of the cherubs, for instance, seems suggestive of pedophilia).

Horseback Riders
Block 7, ground-floor
washroom
Main Camp
H: 30 inches
W: 102 inches

Cherubs Bathing
Block 7, ground-floor
washroom
Main Camp
H: 32 inches
W: 22 inches

Kittens
Block 7, ground-floor
washroom
Main Camp
H: 22 inches
W: 44 inches

TYPHUS WARNING POSTER

The original version of this image was a linoleum-block print made in an edition of about 300 and meant to serve as a warning against lice. The artist, Mieczyslaw Koscielniak, explained in a phone conversation that the poster was commissioned by Oberscharführer Reinicke and made under the direction of SS man Reck. The louse was drawn from nature, that is, from microscopic examination, accounting for the minute detail in its rendition. This version of the poster was copied by one of the camp artists onto the wall.

Although Koscielniak denied any subversive intent, this work seems terribly ironic. Lice were a widespread phenomenon in the camp, and it was hard to do much about them in a situation where there was very little water and no resources for disinfection and a clean change of clothes.

Koscielniak is widely known as a concentration-camp artist. His drawings and prints of camp life, many of which were made during his imprisonment and smuggled out of the camp, have been seen in galleries and publications around the world.[11]

An appropriate postscript to this series of images of "art to order" is this short passage from Primo Levi's *Se questo e un uomo* (Survival in Auschwitz):

"For many weeks I considered these warnings about hygiene as pure examples of the Teutonic sense of humor. . . . But later I understood that their unknown authors, perhaps without realizing it, were not far from some very important truths. In this place it was practically pointless to wash every day in the turbid water of the filthy washbasins for the purpose of cleanliness and health; but it was most important as a symptom of remaining vitality, and necessary as an instrument of moral survival."[12]

*Typhus
Warning
Poster
"One louse,
your death"
Block 18,
basement wall
Main Camp
H: 18 inches*

BLACK HUMOR

The struggle to maintain one's own humanity and the humanity of one's fellow inmates in the concentration camp was a herculean task. Yet in a situation in which art might seem to be the first piece of superfluous baggage to dispense with, it was, in fact, art that helped keep prisoners' spirits alive. Consequently, the camp inmates went to great lengths to protect their artists, who would often perform the relatively easy task of producing paintings, portraits and postcards for the Nazis. At night, they would clandestinely create documentary, often satirical works. These were usually made on small pieces of paper or canvas, and sometimes smuggled out of the camp.

A few satirical pieces were done on walls, and their overt creation sheds light on the nature of humor itself. How could the Nazis have allowed something like "The Chimney Sweep" or "The Apothecary" to be made? The answer, I believe, lies in the totalitarian mind's schizophrenic perception of reality: on the one hand, it sees threats where there are none; on the other, it insists on one-dimensional readings, which blind it, perhaps intentionally, to layered meanings. One can imagine an SS man grinning appreciatively at the frustrated apothecary, who just does not have enough medicine in his shop.

But the intention of these works is not to get a grin out of the SS men. Their purpose is to tell, wreathed and encoded in satire, the truth about Auschwitz.

THE CHIMNEY SWEEP

This painting was probably made by chimney sweeps, since it is located in a basement area that they occupied. These were the chimney sweeps for the prison blocks in Auschwitz I, the main camp. The irony lies in the fact that the chimney sweep is, in Eastern Europe, a symbol of good luck, while the sinister "Oh!!! Oh!!" coming from his mouth indicates that what he sees is anything but lucky. The numbers on the wall are probably those of the artists: B-14286 was a Slovakian Jew named Viktor H. Schick, who was sixteen years old and was liberated by the Russians; A-16053 was Bizo Belo, a Hungarian Jew, also sixteen years old, who last figures in the camp records on January 10, 1945, and may also have survived.[13]

The Chimney Sweep
Block 17, basement
Main Camp
H: 26 inches
W: 48 inches

THE ELEGANT BATHROOM

The origin of this painting is described in detail in the opening chapter. It could just as well have been in the section on Art to Order, but because the artist expressed a consciously ironic intent, it fits well here. The louse-warning poster is equally ironic, but because the artist says he intended it literally, it is included in the previous chapter.

The Elegant Bathroom:
Painting Simulating
Bathroom Mirror,
by Lucjan Motyka
Block 8, second-floor
washroom
Main Camp
H: 42 inches

CHILDREN'S BARRACKS PAINTINGS

The origin of these paintings is explained in the following statement by Eulalia Kurdej, a Warsaw resident and former Auschwitz prisoner:

"The sight of Warsaw in flames was terrible. Corpses lay everywhere. At the Western Station they loaded us onto the trains on which we were brought to Auschwitz, where we arrived on August 12, 1944. It was night, the SS men were moving about on the ramps, and lamps were glowing all around. That was how I found myself in Block 16. Mother was in Block 17, and I was in Block 16, where they kept only children, from the ages of two to fourteen in the case of girls, two to ten in the case of boys. There were about 800 children there. But the children were not entirely without care. Both men and women prisoners took care of us, insofar as they were able.

"One of the nicest recollections of that period was the lovely, selfless gesture of an unknown prisoner, probably a Jew, who, on one occasion when he was repairing something in our barracks, painted for us, on two opposite walls, a school with the word *Schule*, and on the other side, toys."[14]

The meaning of these two paintings eluded me for some time, until I considered the fact that they were done by a Jewish artist. That the faces of these children are so devoid of any expression of joy led me to believe that what was being suggested, if not actually represented, was the march of the Jewish children to their deaths in the gas chambers.

The transports of Jews (which arrived daily, with numbers ranging from 1,000 to 4,000) sometimes consisted almost entirely of women and children, and sometimes only of children. In order to keep the children quiet, they were allowed to carry their toys with them into the gas chambers.

At the time that these particular paintings were made, in August or September of 1944, the family camp of Theresienstadt had already been liquidated. There, paintings of Disney and Hans Christian Andersen characters by Hanna Gottliebowa decorated the walls,[15] and a school had been organized for the children. The fate of these children must have been known to the man who made these paintings.

The murals can be seen along the tourist route in Birkenau.

Children Playing
(left side)
Block 16, Camp Bla,
Children's Barracks,
Women's Camp,
Birkenau
H: 48 inches
W: 144 inches

*Child Going to School
(right side)
Block 16, Camp Bla,
Children's Barracks,
Women's Camp,
Birkenau
H: 48 inches
W: 144 inches*

HITLER AND MUSSOLINI CARICATURES

These may be nothing more than offhand doodling, but the fact that they were found together on nearby pillars, in an attic that could not have been used for much more than storage, suggests that a prisoner may have taken advantage of a moment's free time to dash off these profiles of the two dictators.

Hitler Caricature
Block 8, attic, left side
Main Camp
H: 18 inches

Mussolini Caricature
Block 8, attic, right side
Main Camp
H: 18 inches

PIGEON WITH MESSAGE

This pigeon, carrying a letter marked with a swastika, is located on the wall of one of the "bunker" cells in the basement of Block 11. Perhaps the inmate was thinking of sending a letter home through the camp mail, or fantasizing the arrival of some news —maybe a pardon?

Pigeon with Message
Block 11, Cell 26
Main Camp
H: 3 inches
W: 4 inches

SMILING MAN IN CAMP UNIFORM

This whimsical sketch was found in a most unlikely place, in one of the basement, or bunker, cells of Block 11, the notorious Death Block. Prisoners from these cells were often "selected" to be taken out and shot.

The drawing was, unfortunately, destroyed recently by a film crew that carelessly painted over several cells in Block 11. Despite the good that may come out of making films about Auschwitz, I see no reason outside of pure economics to justify using this place as a film set.

Smiling Man in Camp
Uniform
Block 11, Cell 12
Main Camp
H: 7 inches

THE APOTHECARY

This rather openly satirical painting was made by Tadeusz Mysz-kowski, an Auschwitz artist who painted and sculpted both re-alistic and satirical scenes throughout his stay in the camp. Born on September 25, 1912, in Zakopane, Poland, he studied at the State School of Decorative Arts in Krakow. In 1940, he was arrested in Zakopane, then moved to Tarnow, and on June 14, 1940, to Auschwitz. In 1944, he was sent to Oranienburg, and then to a subcamp of Sachsenhausen. From 1946 to 1951, he worked as director of the art workshop at the Auschwitz museum. In 1961, he emigrated from Poland to Israel, where he died on June 21, 1980.[16]

The man represented in this painting is Czeslaw Ciesielski, the pharmacist of the camp hospital, which was housed in Block 28.[17] The painting is located in that block, in a small attic room that was used to sort and store medicines taken from the people sent to the gas chambers. It was in this building that prisoners too sick to be cured were "spritzed," that is, given injections of phenol directly into the heart. Their corpses were stacked in the basement, sprinkled with chlorine and eventually carted off to the crematorium. Periodic selections separated the seriously ill from those more likely to survive; the unfortunate sick ones were sent to the gas chambers.

The simplest explanation of this scene (perhaps the one used to justify it to the SS men) is that it represents an old pharmacist who is worried about the lack of medicine. Perhaps he has been having a nip at the bottle in his hand and is suffering a hangover.

In fact, the old man represents the pseudoscience of the Third Reich, which sought a chemical cure for the world's ills by exterminating the unwanted members of the population. But de-spite all their efforts, the experiment has failed. The old doctor

The Apothecary
Block 28, attic
Main Camp
H: 48 inches
W: 96 inches

is still looking for the right medicine, but fate (the black cat) holds sway, the death's-head grins in amusement, and the spider continues to weave its web.

FANTASIES

"The paintings were the equivalent of what we didn't have. A man in prison thinks of mountains and space, so I painted a mountain landscape. Everyone thought of space."

This is how Lucjan Motyka described and explained the many idyllic concentration-camp paintings, whose gentle subject matter seems in sharp contradiction to their surroundings.

Two kinds of subject matter seem to predominate: landscapes and images of plenitude. A still life with a bottle of wine, a nude woman carrying a basket of fruit on her head, deer, rabbits munching cabbages—all are images of a paradise regained in art. There are also several voyaging images—a ship and a series of camels and pyramids—that represent dreams of escape in space and time.

In normal times the artist probes the dark corners of the psyche for fantastic visions of the world, but in the concentration camp the relationship is inverted: reality is surrealistic and these simple, even kitschy images serve as an anchor in the chaos of a distorted consciousness.

MOTYKA'S LANDSCAPES

See the opening chapter for the author's account of the making of these two images.

Landscape,
by Lucjan Motyka
Block 8, second-floor washroom
Main Camp
H: 44 inches   W: 64 inches

Tatra Landscape,
by Lucjan Motyka
Block 8, second-floor washroom
Main Camp
H: 44 inches   W: 64 inches

59

UNSIGNED FANTASIES

Mountain Landscape
Block 18, basement
Main Camp
H: 40 inches

Woman Carrying Fruit
Basket
Block 15, attic
Main Camp
H: 14 inches

Still Life with Wine
Bottle
Block 1, attic
Main Camp
H: 15.5 inches
W: 23 inches

Deer
Block 16, ground floor
Main Camp
H: 40 inches

RABBITS EATING CABBAGES

Rabbits Eating
Cabbages,
signed Rubin Franz
Block 15, basement
Main Camp
H: 44 inches
W: 74 inches

The barely visible signature in the lower right-hand corner identifies the artist. Rubin Franz was a Czechoslovakian Jew who arrived at Auschwitz on April 23, 1943. His fate is unknown.[18]

GERMAN RURAL SCENE

This painting is a good example of the kind of bourgeois kitsch that was clearly meant to please the German overseers.

German Rural Scene
Block 1, attic
Main Camp
H: 29 inches
W: 42 inches

DRAWINGS SIGNED KAJZER MAX

These two rather primitive "landscapes," side by side, are signed "Kajzer Max." The same name appears under one of the calendars shown in a later chapter, in which the word for "Help" is misspelled. There are also phonetic spellings and misspellings in the drawing of the town of Auschwitz. This leads to the conclusion that Max was semiliterate.

Prisoners were sometimes assigned to work details in the town of Auschwitz, and the right drawing may represent the prisoner's recollection of the town's layout.

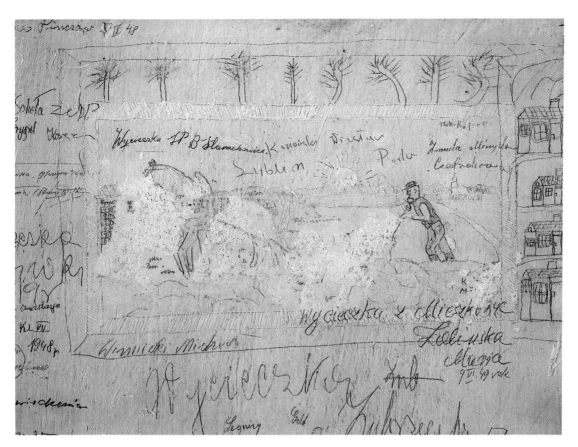

Autobiographical
Landscape,
signed Kajzer Max
Block 11, Cell 26,
left side
Main Camp
H: 14.5 inches

Drawing of the Town
of Auschwitz,
signed Kajzer Max
Block 11, Cell 26,
right side
Main Camp
H: 14.5 inches

CAMELS AND PYRAMIDS

This is one of ten such images found near each other in the stairwell of Block 14, which now houses the Soviet exhibit. When I found them, they were covered by panes of glass that had been painted over. These have now been removed and replaced with clear panes, so the images are visible to tourists.

This is the one example in this book of a kind of decorative painting that was fairly widespread in Auschwitz, by which the walls were adorned with stripes, "marbling" and repeated patterns of various kinds, often stenciled. Here the man plowing and the palm tree have been made with one stencil, the pyramids with another. Both are repeated in the ten images, but in varying relationship to each other.

Camels and Pyramids
Block 14, ground floor
Main Camp
H: 20 inches
W: 26 inches

CRUISE SHIP

This dream of escape is located on the wall of the block functionary's room in Block 11. It can presently be seen by tourists.

Cruise Ship
Block 11
Main Camp
H: 36 inches

BALLERINA

This surprising and incongruous painting was hidden in a storage area, as described in the opening chapter. Nothing is known about the artist or the circumstances surrounding its creation.

Ballerina
Block 18, basement
Main Camp
H: 40 inches

LOVERS

In Auschwitz, it seems impossible to think of anything transcending the cruelties of the struggle for survival—but love could, and occasionally did. The hastily scrawled hearts with names and initials that we are used to seeing on trees, bridges or seemingly inaccessible ledges reverberate here with poignant resonance. At Auschwitz, they almost all signify tragedy.

The simple love of man and woman could either sustain a prisoner in hope or demolish him in despair. On the cell doors of Block 11, I found the words "I love you," but also a poem that begins: "Forget that you loved me. . . ."

The story of the legendary love affair between Edward Galinski, a Pole, and Mala Zimetbaum, a young Jewish woman, who chose death to being separated, is told to this day by Auschwitz survivors; it may be one of the most tragic love stories of all time. Equally moving was the fate of a young SS man, a reluctant participant in the events at Auschwitz, whose love for a Jewish girl from Theresienstadt inspired him to risk his life, and then lose it. In both of these cases, the ennobling, awesome power of love transcended the horror.

NUDE WITH FLOWERS, HEART WITH NAME, CUPID'S HEART

The creators of these drawings, all found in the basement of Block 11, are unknown. There are also numerous smaller, less legible hearts and the words "I love you" in several places in the cells of Block 11.

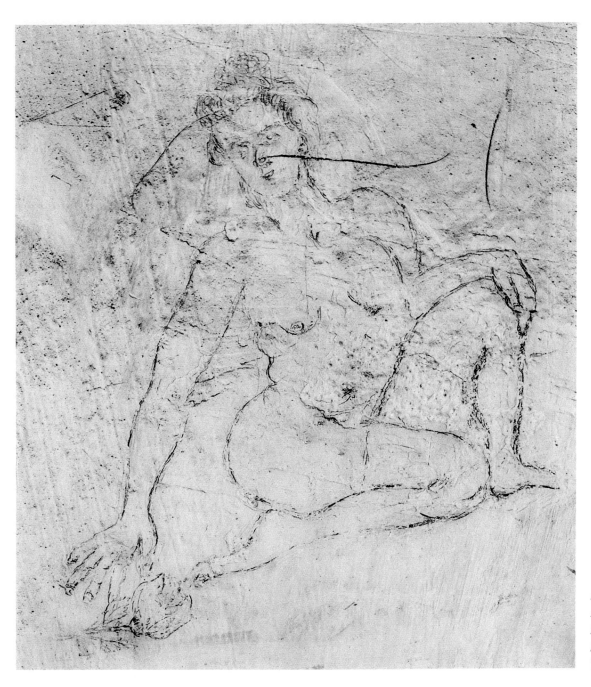

Nude with Flower
Block 11, Cell 24
Main Camp
H: 9.5 inches
W: 8 inches

Heart with Name
Block 11, Cell 11
H: 1.5 inches

Cupid's Heart
with Names
Block 11, Cell 6
Main Camp
H: 5 inches
W: 5 inches

EDEK AND MALLY:
AN AUSCHWITZ LOVE STORY

In several of the bunker cells of Block 11 (17, 18, 19, 20, 23 and 26), there appear a pair of names: Edward Galinski and Mala Zimetbaum. In one of the cells, only the letters MA and the word "Milosc" remain. These are the last traces of one of the most remarkable stories to come out of the Holocaust, and one of the most tragic love stories of all time.

Edward Galinski (Edek) was one of the first prisoners taken to Auschwitz. In the spring of 1940, he was arrested by the Gestapo, with a group of Polish high-school students. They were accused of nothing more than belonging to the intelligentsia or of trying to join the Polish army in France. On June 14, he arrived at Auschwitz and was assigned the number 531.

Mala Zimetbaum (Mally) was born in Brzesk, but emigrated with her family to Antwerp. There, she was arrested for being Jewish, and arrived at Birkenau on September 17, 1942. More than eighty percent of the people in her transport were immediately sent to the gas chambers, including nearly her entire family. She, however, was judged fit for work and assigned the number 19880.

Edek, meanwhile, was doing well by Auschwitz standards. With the help of friends, he had managed to get work in the camp machine shop. This meant that he had a roof over his head, and lighter work than those assigned to the murderous work details. In addition, his overseer was one of the few SS men who did not torture prisoners. Edek was beginning to think of ways to get himself transferred from the main camp to Birkenau, only three kilometers away, where he figured the chances of escape might be better.

Mala had been in Birkenau for over a year when Edek was finally transferred to one of the kommandos there. By the middle of February 1944, Edek had convinced an SS man to supply him

Names on Wall,
by Edward Galinski
Block 11, Cell 20
Main Camp
H: 4 inches
W: 12 inches

with a uniform and a gun. The escape was set for June, when the grain would be tall and the chance of success better. A nearby hideout was arranged with a local man who also had a cousin in Zakopane, near the border, where Edek could hide before attempting to cross into Czechoslovakia.

But fate was to intervene in a wonderful, yet terribly cruel way. His work in a repair crew took him to the women's camp, where he met Mally. Edek was a tall and handsome young man, and Mally's large brown eyes and girlish smile charmed even her SS woman-overseer, who gave her easy work as a messenger. Edek and Mally fell in love.

Edek eventually let his secret be known to the friend with whom he had planned the escape, Wojciech Kielar. He started talking about Mally, saying that sooner or later she would share the fate of all Jews—the gas chamber. When Edek said he was "attached" to her, Kielar knew that he meant he was in love. Kielar gave his place in the escape plan to Mally.

On June 24, 1944, Edek put on the SS uniform; Mally, a worker's frock. With papers and passes stolen by Mally, they passed through the gates of Birkenau. As Kielar wrote in *Anus Mundi*, his autobiographical account of life in Auschwitz, there was only one subject of conversation in the camp that day: Edek and Mally. Their names had become synonymous with freedom.

At first everything went well. They were hidden by Antoni Szymlak, the local man who had promised them a hideout. Then they made their way, without incident, toward Slovakia, where Mally had relatives.

On July 6, 1944, their luck ran out. Mally, walking ahead, was captured by a German border patrol. Edek remained unnoticed and could have made good his escape. Instead, he chose to surrender, to be with Mally.

Edek and Mally were taken back to Auschwitz and imprisoned in the isolation cells in the basement of Block 11. Thanks

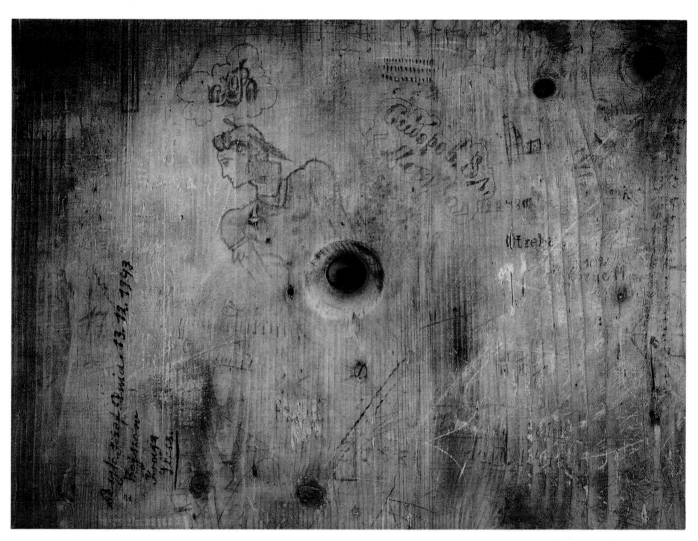

Drawing of
Mala Zimetbaum
Block 11, Cell 23, door
Main Camp
H: 14.5 inches

to Jakub Kozielczuk, the cellkeeper in Block 11, they were able to meet there. One prisoner, Zbigniew Kaczkowski, recalls another method they had of communicating: "Every night, pressing his lips up to a crack in the door, Edek would whistle a certain melody; he would get a reply, the same melody, from Mally in a distant cell." Edek was kept in cells 17, 18, 19, 20, 21, 23, and 26, and in each of them he left both their names; in cells 18, 20 and 23, he drew a likeness of Mally. Despite the torture to which they were subjected, neither of them betrayed any of those connected with their escape.

Two gallows were set up on the same day—one in the women's camp and one in the men's camp. Escapees were normally executed in public in order to discourage other prisoners from attempting escape. In this case, however, the exemplary executions did not go quite as the SS had planned.

Edek stepped up on the stool under the hangman's noose and, just as one of the SS men started reading the sentence, stuck his head in the noose and jumped off the stool. Not to be cheated in this way, his executioners grabbed him, set him back up on the stool and loosened the noose. Once again the sentence was read, first in German, then in Polish. In the moment of silence following the reading, Galinski suddenly cried out in a choked voice: "Long live Pol . . . !" As the noose closed around his neck, an anonymous voice shouted out from among the prisoners: "Hats off!" and the entire camp, as one, removed caps in a defiant salute.

Mally, too, was to make one last desperate attempt to snatch her life out of the hands of the Nazis. As she stood on the gallows, she pulled out a razor and slashed her wrists, but, like Edek, she was not permitted to die by her own hand. As one of the SS men approached her, she slapped him with her bloodied palms, at which several SS men jumped on her and trampled her in front of the whole camp. She died on the way to the crematorium.[19]

Drawing of Mala Zimet-
baum, with Russian
Prisoners' Graffiti
Block 11, Cell 18
Main Camp
H: 13 inches (head)

The Russian inscriptions in the photograph of Mala's portrait on a cell wall read:

twice escaped from the lager
Here sat the Russian Mihail Antonov from the Volhovysk
    region (Byelorussia)
village Zhayeuki near Podbira, Odessa
Misha has been here 20 days
Mitia 8/11/44
We're waiting, we don't know what will be
Whoever was here will not forget, whoever was not
    here [illegible]

Aside from the Jews, the lot of the Russian prisoners of war was by far the worst of any group. The deadly Cyklon B gas was first tried out on 600 Russian prisoners of war and 250 Poles. In March of 1942, only 945 Russian prisoners of war remained out of 12,000 who had been brought to the camp a few months earlier.

Letters "MA" (Mala)
and the Word "Milosc"
(Love) on Peeling
Plaster
Block 11, Cell 26
Main Camp
H: 7 inches
W: 3.5 inches

ESCAPE FROM AUSCHWITZ

The faint signature "V. Pestek" on the middle of the door of cell 26 is that of Victor Pestek, an SS man whose love for a Jewish girl resulted in one of the few successful escapes from Auschwitz.

The story of Victor Pestek and Siegfried Lederer is told by Erich Kulka in a recently published English translation of a book originally printed in Czechoslovakia,[20] so I will present only a condensed version of their story here. I managed to relate the signature to this story only at the very end of my project, while cross-checking a list of names found in the cells of Block 11 against a list of names of known resistance figures in the camp.

Victor Pestek was a reluctant participant in the extermination of Jews at Auschwitz. A German who had grown up in Romania, he had fought on the Eastern Front, was wounded, awarded the Iron Cross, and then sent to what was considered a less-demanding post, Auschwitz. There he fell in love with Rene Karen, a Jewish girl in the Theresienstadt family camp in Birkenau, and proposed to her that they escape together. Rene refused to leave without her mother, so Pestek began looking around for another partner (his escape plan now required one), intending to come back later to try to save Rene and her mother.

Siegfried Lederer, a friend of Rene's father, was at first cautious when Pestek proposed escape; on more than one occasion, an SS man had offered to help a prisoner and then betrayed him. Lederer finally believed Pestek when he said he wanted to escape because he "hated to see women and children murdered."

On April 15, 1944, Lederer and Pestek walked out of the camp, with Lederer dressed in an SS uniform. The two boarded a train, and at noon the next day were in Prague. Through a network of friends, Lederer managed to evade the Gestapo, who were soon on the lookout for him. Pestek, meanwhile, spent his

Victor Pestek's Signature
Block 11, Cell 26, door
Main Camp
H: 14 inches

time carousing with German soldiers about to leave for the front, in order to rifle their pockets for documents that might be useful.

Lederer's goal was to warn the Jewish community in Theresienstadt of the fate that awaited them in Auschwitz, but the Jews in the ghetto found it hard to believe him; they had just received a batch of postcards from the Theresienstadt Jews in Auschwitz! This was a common ploy used by the Nazis, with which they were able to mask their crimes.

On May 25, Lederer and Pestek got on a train to Auschwitz, with a clever plan to free Rene and her mother. Pestek went a few stations farther, to pick up some money he had left with a woman in Myslowice. The two men were to meet the following evening at the station.

Kulka describes what happened:

"Lederer got off. He went through the streets of the town and found accommodations at a hotel. In the morning, he checked around the town and learned that nothing had changed in the family camp. He rang up the SS transport department. The officer confirmed that there would be a car at his disposal. He again checked the whole plan. Everything seemed to be going well. He returned to the hotel, ordered a glass of vodka, and asked for the railway timetable. He looked for the evening train from Myslowice. A quarter of an hour before its scheduled arrival, he was waiting for Pestek on the ramp.

"Shortly before the train arrived, he heard the roar of motorcycles. They stopped in front of the building. A dozen armed SS soldiers emerged from the dust. They closed the railway station and forced all passengers to the waiting room. An assault squad occupied the platform.

"As the train came into the station, Lederer could see Pestek leaning out of the window, looking for him. The commander of the squad apparently recognized him. He jumped up on the steps of Pestek's car and Lederer heard a shot. A grenade exploded on the platform among the SS. Lederer seized the opportunity. He made for the motorcycles in front of the station. They were not being watched. He mounted the first in the row, started the engine, and accelerated. In forty minutes he reached the Czech frontier, 50 km. from Auschwitz."

Pestek apparently escaped this time. Kulka quotes another survivor, Josef Neumann, who told him:

"I was going through the camp gate, when an SS barracks leader came up and searched me thoroughly. I felt him shove a note into my pocket, which turned out to be from Pestek, telling me where to meet him. I went to the unfinished 'Mexico' camp in section B-III and found Pestek hiding in an attic, pointing two revolvers at me.

" 'Maybe now you'll trust me,' he said. I embraced him, for his return seemed miraculous. He told me, 'If you want to come with me, get ready, we leave at 10:30.' I think he had a car behind the camp. He asked me to see that Rene from the Czech Family Camp was also ready. It was probably mainly on her account that he had dared to return to Birkenau.

"I was on my way to the appointed place, fully prepared for flight. But I noticed something unusual going on at the barracks where Pestek was hiding. He had been betrayed and was surrounded by the SS, so I continued on to the Czech Family Camp to warn Rene.

"Scarcely had I done this when I heard them looking for me all over the camp. Three SS members who were especially noted for their brutality, one on a motorcycle, were combing the camp, searching every block. Their first question when they found me was, 'Where's Pestek?'

" 'I don't know,' I said, an answer that immediately cost me two teeth. They kicked me along to the guardroom, where I saw Pestek hanging by his wrists from the bars of the window. He was so bloody from beatings he was barely recognizable. They tied me by my wrists to the other window and left us alone together for a while, hoping perhaps to overhear our conversation through the door.

"Then they tied Pestek and me together and dragged us to the notorious Block 11 at the Auschwitz main camp, where people slated for execution were held. It must have been a grim sight as the bleeding SS officer and the Jewish prisoner, lashed together, entered the block from which few ever came out alive. Pestek and I were separated and thrown into solitary confinement.

"Jakub Kozelcik [Neumann's spelling], the Jewish prison capo, gave me daily reports on what was happening with Pestek, and once he let me briefly meet with Pestek in his cell. He looked bad, cruelly treated. He only said, 'I disclosed nobody. Lederer is o.k.' Kozelcik, who had experience and connections, kept trying to convince me that he could save my life if I paid a considerable sum to the SS dealing with the case. With Jakub's help I obtained the money from my friends in the camp, and he paid it secretly to the SS as a ransom.

"Pestek was interrogated viciously for a month, undergoing fearful torture and violence. He was sentenced by SS Polizeigericht Katowice to death and was shot.[21]

"From Jakub we learned how Pestek had fearlessly threatened the SS who questioned him, for he knew a great deal about most of them. Thus he had to be silenced."

Neumann was transferred to a work camp in Bavaria, where he was liberated by the U.S. Army. Lederer returned to Theresienstadt to head the resistance movement there, and also managed to get a report on conditions in Auschwitz to the International Red Cross in Switzerland. He then joined a partisan band in Slovakia, where he was wounded. He survived the war, though, and died on April 15, 1972, at the age of sixty-eight. As for Rene, she was transferred to a camp near Hamburg and, after the war, moved to the United States with her mother.

HEROES

Ordinary concepts of heroism fail when it comes to describing what went on in the concentration camps. Physical and moral survival became impossible for many, who had to choose either death or a life in which survival was the only remaining value. Many of the camp's real heroes are those who chose to die rather than survive on unacceptable terms.

The words "Abandon hope all ye who enter here," from Dante's *Inferno*, may have been a prisoner's piece of fatalistic advice, but a refusal to abandon hope may be the only criterion for heroism in a concentration camp. The survivor-hero, as Sidra DeKoven Ezrahi observes in *The Holocaust in Literature*, "is one who resists his condition as a victim."[22]

Jakub Kozielczuk, the cellkeeper in Block 11, who helped and saved hundreds of people due to his privileged position, is typical of the concentration-camp hero. He chose to survive, so that he could do good whenever possible, though that meant being involved in unavoidable evil; his position required him to lead prisoners to the Death Wall to be shot.

The choice of the many resistance fighters who were captured was simpler—talk or die. For the most part, they kept their silence, and paid the price. The Polish romantic tradition, dating back to the eighteenth century, provided a continuum with which many could identify. Faced with death, these people knew themselves to be heroes, and stoically left behind their marks as a way of affirming the value of their lives and inspiring others.

"ABANDON HOPE ALL YE WHO ENTER HERE"

Although there is no record of who may have made this inscription, one prisoner who was held in this cell in the fall of 1943 recalls seeing it when he was imprisoned there:

"Twelve of us were locked in Cell 8, the corridor cell without a window. There was nothing in the cell except for a toilet bucket and a small grated light bulb. We started looking around and saw that it was dirty, with bloodstains on the wall. In one place we read the words of Dante: 'Abandon Hope All Ye Who Enter Here.' And on the wooden door there was the inscription, 'condemned to death by starvation,' with ten or so marks after it—these were the days of his life."[23]

This is one of several instances in which prisoners quoted passages from well-known literary works or left behind terse philosophical comments. These show prisoners trying to understand their concentration-camp experience by placing it within the context of familiar worldviews. Primo Levi recounts how one day, while carrying the soup ration to his group, he suddenly began quoting from the *Divine Comedy*. He found this to be a turning point; from that moment he began to recover his identity as a man.[24]

Line from
Dante's Inferno
"Abandon Hope All Ye
Who Enter Here"
Block 11,
Cell 8, doorjamb
Main Camp
H: 2.5 inches

95

THE CELLKEEPER

This drawing is located in one of the cells in the basement of Block 11. The heavyset character with the keys is reminiscent of the portrait of Jakub Kozielczuk, the Block 11 cellkeeper, that was made by Stefan Jasienski on the door of Cell 21. Thinking that this might be another drawing of the cellkeeper, I went to Jan Pilecki, the surviving recordkeeper of Block 11, to find out what I could about this person. The ensuing interview brought to light a remarkable story, so I present it here in full. Could this be Jakub Kozielczuk, I asked?

"Yes, this is Jakub Kozielczuk, especially because of the powerful build, and because he is holding keys, and, besides the SS men, the cellkeeper was the only one in the bunker who had the keys. There was no one else as large as he was. He was tremendous, because he had been a wrestler. He also went about in the summertime without a shirt, as he is in this drawing.

"Block 11, as you know, had several different functions. The basement had cells, and was called 'the bunker.' On the main floor there were rooms for the block officials, and I had a room there, while on the second floor there was quarantine, for people coming and going.

"The most important person in the block was the cellkeeper, the person who serviced the bunker. When I came to Block 11, the cellkeeper was a Silesian Pole named Hannes, which is Silesian for John. He was close to the SS men and terrorized everyone. He was not a good person, and so there was not much that could be done for the people imprisoned in the block. Hannes stole from the prisoners, and penalized people for not reacting quickly enough to his commands by taking away their food rations and sharing them with the SS men.

"Then one fine day, about December 1942—I can't remem-

The Cellkeeper
Block 11, Cell 24
Main Camp
H: 21 inches
W: 16 inches

97

ber exactly—Rapportführer Palitsch came to Block 11 with a huge prisoner. We all looked at him in amazement, because this was the largest person we had ever seen. Palitsch talked with the block führer and went out. The block führer told us this would be the new cellkeeper, along with Hannes. Everyone was terrified! But slowly I began making contact with him and learned that he was a very interesting person. He had no idea what a concentration camp was or where he was! How did he get here, I asked him. It took him some time to trust me, and I him, but I'll tell you the story as I finally learned it.

"Jakub was a Polish Jew who had emigrated to the U.S. He had been a professional wrestler in a circus in the U.S., and came with this circus to Europe and Poland. He was to have returned with them after the tour—this was in August 1939—but he fell in love with a girl from a town named Krynki, near Bialystok, where he originally came from. Then the war broke out and he couldn't leave, and he was stuck in the ghetto. When the time came to liquidate the ghetto, the Nazis sent everyone to Auschwitz. So what saved Jakub?

"It turns out that among his papers he had a letter from the champion German boxer Max Schmeling, and an autographed photograph of himself with Schmeling.

"In his day he had been a bodyguard for either Al Capone or one of his rivals—I don't remember which. At that time, there was the world championship boxing match between Joe Louis and Max Schmeling. Schmeling, you know, was a half god to the Germans. And those that financed Schmeling in the U.S. gave him bodyguards during his stay there. One of them was Jakub Kozielczuk. After the first match, Schmeling apparently wrote a letter to the organizers, thanking them, and also thanking Jakub personally.

"The Germans had a tremendous respect for strength, and Schmeling was a god, so they decided to find some way to reward

Jakub for this and at the same time make use of him for their ends. They thought they would have their man in the bunker and that he would tell them everything. This is what Jakub told me after he began to trust me. There also was a Jew in the camp named Abram that came to Jakub and spoke to him in broken Spanish. They had known each other before in Havana. Jakub spoke several languages, but none of them well.

"When I discovered that he was a good guy and that the Nazis wanted to use him as a stool pigeon, I decided to do something about it. The first matter that had to be taken care of was the other cellkeeper. What I did was this: When transports of civilian police prisoners came, all their effects were taken away in Block 11 and stored in the attic. Since most of them went before the court and were shot, Hannes, as I soon learned, took their things and gave them to the SS men. When I knew that Hannes had taken something, I took Jakub aside and told him that I wanted to do good for people, and told him that if he wanted to be able to help people here, he would have to gain the confidence of the people in the political section. You could tell them, I said, that you're new here, but you told me to report, so I'm telling you that the cellkeeper has been taking rings and things and keeping them somewhere and giving them to the SS men. Jakub did as I said; a group came from the political section and found the necessary items where Jakub had said they would be, and Hannes was sent to another block. They also changed the block führer, another one came, and then a new life started. Thanks to Jakub it was possible to do what had to be done. There were some decent people then and our friends in the camp could find out what was going on in Block 11. We could smuggle notes in and out, and even food.

"How did Jakub manage to do all this? Sometimes there were problems because he would get the numbers of the cells mixed up. But he did everything at great danger to himself and was indeed extraordinary, to such a degree that he himself suffered greatly in our block. The saddest thing was the so-called cleaning-out of the bunker, or the sitting of the summary court. This occurred when the bunker was filled, when there were a hundred, or even two hundred, people in the bunkers. Then people from the political section came along with the camp leaders and block führer and dragged the prisoners from the cells, undressed them in the bathroom and took them out and shot them. The summary court was held once or twice a month and usually concerned political prisoners.

"During these times Jakub went about half-conscious. This was his saddest role. He felt this all very deeply. It was his job to lead the naked prisoners marked for death right up to the Death Wall. This was a terrible time for Jakub, and he had to drink at least half a liter of grain alcohol to be able to do this. Because Jakub was, you could say, the uncrowned king of the Jews in the camp, they gave him everything he wanted. For them he was a great person, he could do anything; that's why he was respected so much. My friends, too, knew that everything I did was thanks to Jakub. He had a splendid reputation. The majority of Jews had contacts with other Jews that worked in 'Canada,' which was the kommando where the goods brought in from new transports were sorted out. There were fortunes there. So whatever he wanted he got. And what did he need? He needed to drink. Because he was so huge and strong, he needed a lot of alcohol to get drunk.

"Whenever the SS would come, or when the summary court from Katowice was held, he would walk about with his shirt popping its buttons. The Nazis even permitted him not to wear the Star of David, and the chief of the Gestapo would come up to him and pat him on the back, because it impressed them how strong he was. We got a piece of iron bar from the machine shop, and he did what he used to do in the circus—he twisted the bar with his bare hands. He would shout and grunt the way they do in the circus, and then bend it, and whatever you might say about it being soft metal or whatever, still, three or four normal people couldn't even budge it. The SS men gawked at him in disbelief. When they came they would slap him on the back and say, 'How're you doing, Jakub?' But he had to drink before the executions; otherwise he would have tears in his eyes. That's the way it was with the beatings. He yelled a lot but hardly hit at all. When the SS said to him, 'Jakub, how are you beating?' Jakub, said, 'I do it like a man should.'

"Then there was the time they took him with them to hang some people. This was a terrible experience for him. And when one of the escapees, a Colonel Englas, a Czechoslovakian Jew who escaped from the camp, was caught and sentenced to hang, Jakub was sent out to hang him. He made the noose too long, so that the rope broke. He went to the bunker for that, but fortunately came out okay. [One of the bunker cells in fact has the name 'Kodzielczyk' carved into it, but whether this was a variation on the spelling of Jakub's last name or another prisoner's name is impossible to say.]

"This is the story of a man who did everything he could possibly do in this situation. Thanks to him it was possible to do very much. It is thanks to him that my wife is alive.

"My wife was brought in from Myslowice to appear before the summary court, and that was the equivalent of a death sentence. So I asked Jakub for help. Who else could I have asked? No one else in the whole camp could have done what he did. She was not my wife yet; we fell in love in the camp. Jakub was close to the chief of the Gestapo in the town, who was also a member of the summary court. So when this *Lustige* came up and clapped him on the back, as they all do, Jakub told him what was going on.

"And he saved her. He got her sent not to the court, but to the camp. Jakub didn't tell me everything he had to do, but one of the things he had to organize was a Persian lamb coat that the Gestapo chief wanted for his wife. And he got it. Jakub got it from one of his friends in Canada. It had to be smuggled out of the camp into town. The machinists prepared an oxygen bottle with a special threaded plug so that the coat could be stuffed inside it, and it was arranged that some welding had to be done somewhere to have an excuse to smuggle the bottle out of the camp. This is all thanks to him.

"In 1944, the war situation changed radically and the camp commander changed, the Death Wall was taken down, and I decided to get out of Block 11. I arranged to get sent to the hospital several times, and finally got sent to Block 15. That was when I lost contact with Jakub, in May of 1944. Jakub stayed there. I wanted to get out of the camp as soon as possible. I was afraid to stay there, because I was one of the people they called 'a bearer of secrets,' and that was dangerous. So some of my friends managed at the last minute to get me signed onto one of the first transports in late November. Jakub stayed to the end. I searched for him everywhere after the war and inquired abroad. I heard a lot of different things, that he was in Israel, that he had died, but I never found out for certain.

"I remember him and will always remember him with a great deal of feeling. I owe him a lot. He did as much as it was possible to do in Block 11."

Another survivor, Leon Mackiewicz of Warsaw, states that Jakub Kozielczuk, widely known as "Kuba," was sent to Leitmeritz in the middle of November 1944.

Still another survivor, who wishes to remain anonymous, related the following incident: "A certain man who had been sentenced to death broke down at the last moment and offered to give the Germans the names of his fellow conspirators in exchange for his life. Jakub, sensing the danger, gave him a powerful blow, knocking him unconscious. When the SS man asked what had happened, Jakub told him that the man had tried to escape. The German then pulled out his pistol and shot the would-be traitor in the head."

Pilecki also added that "there were situations in which it was necessary to save hundreds of people by killing one. That also had to be done. A stool pigeon was dangerous. Sometimes the Germans would put ten people in a cell with a stool pigeon in among them. If I told Jakub that something needed to be done, he would do it; he trusted me and knew it had to be done. Who else would do it? They would be afraid. It was enough for him just to hit someone a bit too hard. Then he would say it was an accident because the person had been breaking a rule or something."

THE BOXER

Cell 18 in Block 11 is perhaps the most famous cell in Auschwitz, for it was there, in 1979, that Pope John Paul II paid homage to Father Maximilian Kolbe. Father Kolbe, a Franciscan priest who has now been beatified, voluntarily gave his life in place of a man condemned to death by starvation. Over the years, millions of devout Catholics have gone to Father Kolbe's cell to pray, lay flowers and light candles. As a result of all these candles, however, the cell walls are now black with a coating of carbon and tallow, and the inscriptions on them are almost entirely obscured.

It was with some difficulty, then, that I finally found several images underneath this black coating. One of them was a portrait of Mala Zimetbaum, whose story appears earlier. Another image, which I could not figure out for some time, was a barely visible pencil sketch of a boxer. I simply could not imagine what a boxer might have to do with Auschwitz. Then one day I picked up a copy of a recently published autobiography by an Auschwitz prisoner named Tadeusz Sobolewicz, in which the author describes a boxing match that took place in the camp.[25]

Looking into the matter further, I discovered that this boxer's name was Tadeusz Pietrzykowski, and that he now lived in Bielsko-Biala, less than an hour's drive from Auschwitz. I decided to go see him. The boxer in the drawing had a head of clearly drawn curly hair, and I knew that I was on the right track when Pietrzykowski, a short but well-built man with close-cropped curly hair, opened the door.

Tadeusz Pietrzykowski arrived in Auschwitz on June 14, 1940, with the very first transport of Polish political prisoners; he received the number 77. Having fought against the Nazi army that invaded Poland in 1939, he was arrested on the Hungarian-Yugoslavian border while trying to make his way to France. He had intended to join the Polish army there.

The Boxer
Block 11, Cell 18
Main Camp
H: 8.5 inches

"Teddy," as he was known in the boxing world, had begun making a career for himself in the ring and was already the bantamweight champion of Warsaw and Eastern Poland. He was a student of the legendary Polish trainer Felix Stamm, whom Pietrzykowski credits with having made a "gentleman" out of him, by teaching him the meaning of Poland's national motto: "God, Honor, Country."

For Teddy, those words were a source of strength during the dark years, and he never lost hope that someday Poland would emerge victorious. It was this faith that enabled him to survive the first year in the camp; he worked as a carpenter, haymaker, builder, animal caretaker, and even as a massager for the SS, doing, as he says, "anything to survive, but never forgetting the dignity and honor of Poland."

Then on one Sunday in March 1941, while the prisoners were picking lice out of their clothes and killing them by squashing them between their fingernails, Teddy, sitting naked on a pile of bricks, heard a commotion coming from the direction of the camp kitchen and men yelling: "Hit him, hit him!"

A moment later, one of the prisoners ran up saying: "The capos are boxing and I hear that one of you knows how to box!" Teddy tells the story:

"One of my friends pointed at me, so the prisoner said to me, 'So, little guy, you want to earn some bread? Come on and box!'

"Walter Duning, a capo and the German light-middleweight champion before the war, was taking on all comers, beating them all, and had just knocked the teeth out of his previous opponent, the kitchen capo. At that point I weighed only ninety-three pounds, but I decided to fight anyway, despite the warnings of my friends, who tapped their heads as if to show that I was crazy, and said, 'You, he'll kill you, he'll eat you!'

"At the corner of the camp kitchen a square had been built,

at the center of which stood a 'ring,' where the fight was to take place. Opposite me stood Walter Duning, blond, well built, about twice as heavy as I was, with tremendous muscles. I looked at that guy and thought, If I get hit, it's all over. In a thousandth of a second my past flashed before my eyes—Stamm, the ring, my club emblem. But I was hungry, my friends were hungry, and this was a chance to survive. All this was spinning around in my head when Brodniewicz [one of the most notorious functionaries in Auschwitz], who was refereeing, called out: 'Ring free. Fight!'

"I knew that only my brain could save me. I shook hands, then stepped back with a left jab, keeping at a distance and bobbing back and forth from one leg to another. Walter just stood there like a rock and coiled himself up, ready to let me have it—while I just kept dancing around him. Then I started making contact with left jabs, then double and triple jabs. He came at me, and I ducked this way and that just to keep him away from me.

"The Poles, meanwhile, were yelling 'Kill the German,' which was about the dumbest thing they could have done under the circumstances, since some of the functionaries, like Brodniewicz, understood Polish and could have reacted brutally. By this time, though, the boys were cheering, which warmed things up a bit for me and gave me a little strength. The SS men gathered around, laughing.

"During the second round I kept up the same tactics— distance, distance, all the time scoring points with the left. He managed to hit me a couple of times, but I usually don't feel the punches during a fight, and I managed to hold him off.

"In the third round I guess I got him good. Anyway, there was a clinch. I could see there was blood on his face, from either his nose or his lip, and so I didn't hit him, but stopped, waiting to see what he would do.

"The Poles started yelling 'Kill the German, kill the German!' at which point Brodniewicz and the other capos threw themselves on the prisoners watching the fight, and began punching and kicking them.

"Walter, meanwhile, just dropped his hands and smiled at me. When he stopped, I stopped, and we both started laughing.

"Walter threw his arms around me and said, 'Good, very good, young man, come with me.'

"And he took me to the first floor of Block 24, and asked me, 'When was the last time you ate?' 'Yesterday,' I answered. He then gave me a half a loaf of bread and a piece of meat. There I was, surrounded by capos who were beating and murdering my friends, and they were all slapping me on the back. One of them came up to me and asked me where I would like to work, and I of course said the kitchen—there was food there, carrots, turnips and potatoes.

"Anyway, they got me a job in the kitchen and later in the stable, where I did the heaviest work I could find to get myself back into shape. I ate a lot to put on some weight, because the capos and SS wanted me to fight every Sunday.

"The Germans actually set up a lottery on my fights—one would bet ten marks, another one hundred marks. On one occasion an SS man that we called 'Uncle' bet 1,000 marks on me, and won. He asked me what I wanted, and I said, of course, 'Food!' He ordered five huge kettles of soup from the SS kitchen to be given to the prisoners. One Mussulman (a prisoner in the terminal stages of starvation and psychological dehabilitation) was so hungry that he dove right into one of the pots, which, fortunately, was not hot, or he might have scalded himself to death.

"Sometimes there were these capos who used to beat the prisoners in order to impress the SS men. My friends would go up to them and goad them into fighting me, saying, 'Teddy is out of shape.' When I got hold of a guy like that, I would play with him, not knock him out and end the fight. This would give my friends some entertainment, and teach the capo a lesson. Once, I fought with this guy who was a real murderer. I went five rounds with him, and they had to carry him out of the ring. I beat him terribly. His mouth was in shreds. That was a German capo from Mauthausen, and he just couldn't hit me. Interestingly, the Germans didn't take his side; they took mine. They used to call me the White Fog, because nobody could hit me."

Teddy had thirty-seven fights at Auschwitz and won all of them except two matches with a Jewish boxer, Lew Sanders, the Dutch light-middleweight champion. "His wife and children were gassed in Birkenau," Teddy told me. "He was a very good boxer, and in the fight with him I had to make the greatest effort of my life. The fight ended in a draw. Because of this, my opponent got recognition in the eyes of the capo, who gave him bread and a job carrying pots in the kitchen, which allowed him to eat better and survive." Another survivor recalls a rematch, which was won by Sanders, a fight Teddy did not mention;[26] but then, boxers are known for editing out their losses.

Not all of Teddy's fights were inside the ring. Once, while working on a farming kommando, he saw one of the capos beating a prisoner who was down on all fours. Teddy went up to the head of his kommando and told him that he was a boxer and would like to "train" with the capo who was beating the prisoner. The SS men of both details agreed to Teddy's proposition, thinking to have a bit of fun.

Teddy went up to the capo and asked him why he was beating the prisoner. "Shut your mouth, you dumb Polack. Do you want to get it, too?" he said, coming at Teddy. Teddy dropped him with two punches and answered: "How'd you like to go to the crematorium?"

"I don't know how that fight would have ended," Teddy says. "I was just getting ready to give him a really good beating when the prisoner who was being beaten, a man with wire-rimmed glasses held together with string, stood up and said to me, 'Don't beat your brother, my son!'

" 'Bug off,' I said, thinking to myself, Whose son do you think I am, anyway? And I hit the capo on the jaw a third time."

The man with the glasses continued begging him to stop fighting and fell to his knees, grasping his hands, imploring, "Do not fight, my son."

"His face was almost strangely calm," Teddy recalls. "I just didn't know what to say, as if I had no tongue in my mouth. So I just waved my hand, because the break was over and it was time to go back to work."

The man whom Teddy tried to defend was none other than Father Maximilian Kolbe. The two met again, and Kolbe told Teddy to leave to God the job of meting out justice, and also told him about his missionary work in Japan. Teddy gave the priest a piece of bread, and was ready to fight again when he heard that another prisoner had stolen it from him; but again Kolbe would not allow it. When Teddy gave him another piece of bread, Kolbe broke the bread in two, gave half of it to the thief, and said, "He must be hungry, too."

Teddy saw Father Kolbe for the last time in the summer of 1941, when a selection was being made for death by starvation as punishment for the escape of a prisoner. He saw Father Kolbe push his way to the front of the kommando and ask to die in place of another prisoner; and Teddy saw him taken away to Block 11. As fate would have it, it was in Father Kolbe's cell in Block 11 that I found the drawing of Teddy the boxer.

"There was one prisoner who was being beaten by a capo," Teddy said, "and one of my friends came up to me and said, 'They're beating Stasiek,' or Jurek—I don't remember what his name was. Anyway, I went over and said, 'Leave him alone,' and I gave him a piece of bread, or something like that. He was one of those boys that were in every kommando, who knew how to draw a little and would do these illustrated letters that were so popular among the SS, in exchange for cigarettes or a piece of bread. I remember seeing him two or three times before a fight, drawing pictures of me. About half a year later someone came up to me and said that they finished him off in the bunker. I don't know how; I just heard that he died."

In March of 1943, Teddy was transferred to the camp at Neuengamme. He continued his boxing career there, knocking out a German heavyweight named Schally Hodemach in a legendary fight that later became the subject of a book and a film.[27] Teddy is still active as a sports trainer in Bielsko-Biala.

THE COMMANDO

Stefan Jasienski was one of a crack group of 316 Polish commandos dropped into Poland by parachute from Great Britain and Italy between 1941 and 1944. Their tasks were varied, ranging from observation and communication to diversion and sabotage. Jasienski landed in Poland on March 13, 1943, and was assigned to observe German troop movements to the east in Lithuania until November. He then fulfilled various tasks as an underground soldier in Warsaw until July of 1944, when he was assigned to work with the resistance fighters located near the concentration camp at Auschwitz.

Jasienski's task was essentially to act as liaison between the organized underground resistance groups in Auschwitz and the Silesian command of the AK, or Home Army. A decision had been made to prepare for an armed uprising in the camp should the Nazis begin a total liquidation of all the prisoners (who usually numbered about 100,000 at any one time). Only such an extreme situation would justify an uprising; otherwise, the risks and losses would be too great.

In the summer of 1944, Hauptscharführer Otto Moll expressed his willingness to level the camp, thereby murdering all witnesses to the Nazi crimes. Fortunately, this was averted, due largely to the organized underground activity both inside and outside the camp, in which Jasienski played a great part. Information smuggled out of the camp made its way to London, and British broadcasts to the Germans suggested that a massive liquidation of prisoners by the Nazis might be met with reprisals on German prisoners held by the Allies.

Jasienski spent a month working in the Auschwitz area, making contact with the local underground and with the resistance movement within the camp, and familiarizing himself with the

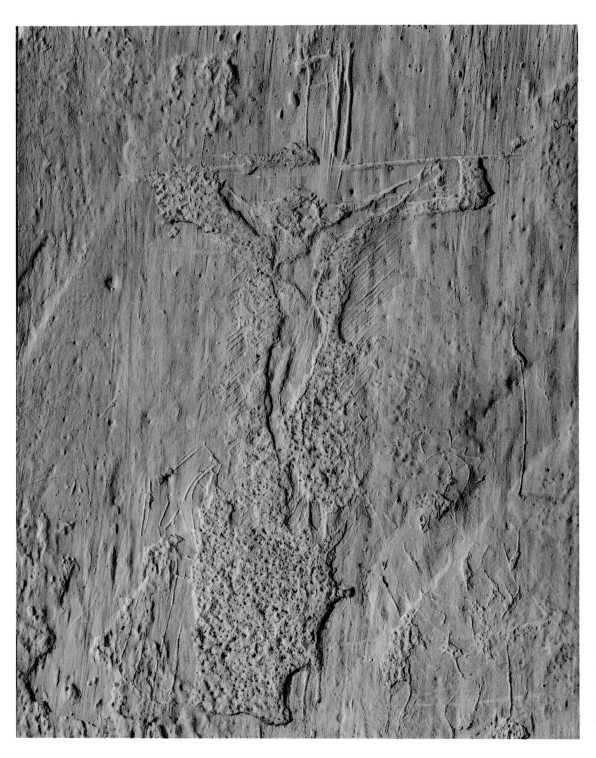

Crucifix,
by Stefan Jasienski
Block 11, Cell 21
Main Camp
H: 6 inches
W: 4 inches

plans for an attack on Auschwitz. On the night of August 28, his luck ran out. He was seriously wounded and captured by a Nazi patrol that was cleaning out resistance elements in the village of Malec. He was taken that same night to Auschwitz, where his capture caused extreme consternation among the underground. It was a serious blow to their plans to liberate the camp through a parachute assault, a plan that, in retrospect, may seem unrealistic, but to which they attached great importance in their desperate situation. And there was also the fear that he knew too much about the identities of the camp conspirators, and might spill the information under torture. But because he knew nothing more than the pseudonyms of the camp conspirators, the decision was apparently made not to murder him preventively.[28] In fact, there was never any indication that he betrayed anyone during his imprisonment.

Jasienski was transferred from the prison hospital in Block 21 to cell 21 in the basement of Block 11, the Death Block. The last mention made of him by the camp underground is in a note dated November 18. A priest attached to the Home Army later claimed to have heard his confession during a brief meeting on December 3.

Most likely, he was executed sometime between January 3 and 8 in 1945. This conclusion is based on a calendar found in cell 21 that lists the numbers 13, 20, 27, 4, 11, 18, 25, and 1, and above them the letter P, standing for *Poniedzialek*, the Polish word for Monday. These numbers were the dates of successive Mondays from November 13, 1944, to January 1, 1945. Two dots are marked after a carefully carved-out "1," and after this the calendar stops.

Besides this calendar, Jasienski left several other reliefs carved into the plaster of the cell wall—a Sacred Heart figure, a crucifix, and a Syrena, the symbol of the city of Warsaw. And on the door of his cell he left a remarkably complete visual

The Sacred Heart,
by Stefan Jasienski
Block 11, Cell 21
Main Camp
H: 16 inches
W: 8.5 inches

autobiography, with items symbolizing various aspects of his life: book, pencil and ruler, for his studies in architecture; the mark of the patriotic Arkonia society, to which he belonged; lance, saber and horse, for his membership in the cavalry; an English Cromwell tank; a greyhound, since he often went to dog races during his training in England; a pouncing eagle, the emblem of his parachutist division; a Halifax bomber and a parachutist, symbolizing his commando activity; his family crest; a wineglass (perhaps a lonely New Year's toast to himself); and a portrait of the cellkeeper, Jakub Kozielczuk.

The riddle of the biography on the cell door was not solved until 1965, when a visitor to the museum noticed the drawings on the door and had a photograph of them sent to the wife of a close friend of Jasienski. She first identified the sign of the Arkonia society, and then noticed the other biographical elements. Historian Adam Cyra pieced together the remaining parts of the story.[29]

Jasienski's cell in the basement of Block 11 is one of the few that can be seen by tourists to the camp museum.

*Commando's
Autobiography,
by Stefan Jasienski
Block 11, Cell 21, door
Main Camp
H: 16 inches
W: 22 inches*

NAME AND INITIALS
OF PIOTR PIATY

Although little is known about this resistance figure, it has been reported that he played a key role in the escape of several important prisoners.

In the summer of 1944, resistance leaders in the camp began fearing that the Germans were planning to liquidate the entire camp in order to wipe out all evidence of their crimes there. An escape was planned in order to strengthen communications with the outside world and to consider what action might be taken if the feared liquidation were to start taking place. The man chosen for the escape was Lucjan Motyka, an artist quoted in the opening chapter, who was then working outside the camp, repainting the camp butcher shop. Nearby was the SS kitchen, where Piotr Piaty worked. Piaty prepared a hideout in the attic of the kitchen, on the theory that no one would think to look for an escapee right under the noses of the enemy. The plan was successfully carried out on July 22, 1944.

After the success of Motyka's escape, it was decided to use the same method again. Two other resistance men, Zbigniew Kaczkowski and Jerzy Sokolowski, were chosen, and on July 28, during a lunch break, they sauntered into the SS kitchen as if they were repairmen and hid in the attic. During their escape, they were spotted by an SS guard. The guard released the safety on his rifle, and then, as Sokolowski later explained:

"When I said farewell to life, something happened which surpassed my imagination and expectation: A soldier of the 'master nation' turned around and slowly walked to the guard tower and lit up a cigarette. Soaking wet, but drunk with freedom, I ran with the remainder of my strength from the barbed wire, the hunger, the smoking crematoria, and the one 'good German' I had run into in my whole life."

*Name and Initials
of Piotr Piaty
Block 11, Cell 21
Main Camp
H: 2 inches
W: 5 inches*

Their freedom lasted only three days. Haggard and emaciated, they were not hard to spot. A seven-year-old *Volksdeutscher* (an ethnic German living in Poland) turned them in, receiving a handful of candies for his deed. Kaczkowski and Sokolowski were beaten and thrown into cells in Block 11 (at the same time as were Edek Galinski and Mally Zimetbaum). Both men, however, were sent to other camps and survived the war.

Piotr Piaty was one of five resistance members caught during an escape attempt at the end of December. He was executed, along with Bernard Swierczyna and the Austrians Ernst Burger, Rudolf Friemel and Ludwig Vesely, in the last hanging that took place in Auschwitz before the camp was liberated.[30]

"LAURA"—ANTONI SZLACHCIC

Antoni Szlachcic was a young member of the resistance from the town of Babice, near Auschwitz. Born on March 2, 1919, he was about to begin studying law when the war broke out. The Germans resettled his family to the town of Auschwitz, where he worked in a darkroom. By the spring of 1940, he was a member of the Home Army resistance group (using the name Laura), and was involved in contacting prisoners in the concentration camp. His brother, Marian Szlachcic, recalls:

"Having access to amateur films brought to him for development by the Gestapo and German soldiers, he secretly created an archive documenting Nazi crimes. He personally took part in receiving air drops, and was engaged in organizing escapes from Auschwitz. On more than one occasion I witnessed conversations setting escape routes and preparing documents, clothes and food."

In the fall of 1942, two men betrayed the Home Army conspiracy, and as a result more than thirty people were captured and executed. Szlachcic managed to avoid capture by pure chance, and continued his activities until the spring of 1944, when he was again betrayed, and this time arrested. In the camp he continued to send notes of encouragement to his compatriots. To Zofia Domasik, a Home Army messenger who was beaten terribly by the Nazis, he wrote: "Zofia, hang on! Soon it will be over." He was sentenced to death on January 5, 1945, at the last sitting of the summary court in Block 11; he was shot the next day near crematorium number 5 in Birkenau.[31]

A few words should be said about the man who sentenced him. Johannes Thummler, now well over eighty, is alive and well in West Germany and has never been brought to justice. From September 1943 to January 1945, he was the chief of the Gestapo in Katowice, and chairman of the summary court that met every

Pseudonym, "Laura,"
and Real Name,
Antoni Szlachcic,
a Resistance Fighter
Block 11, Cell 20, wall
Main Camp
H: 8 inches

*Names of Resistance
Fighters Antoni
Szlachcic and
Konstanty Kempa
(pseudonym "Kostek")
Block 11,
Cell 19, window
Main Camp
H: 18 inches*

few weeks in Block 11 at Auschwitz to judge the "politicals." These were people brought in by the Gestapo from nearby Katowice or Myslowice. They were kept on the first floor and occasionally in the basement, where prisoners from the camp itself were kept before the court decided their fate.

The so-called trials lasted from one to three minutes. No one was ever declared not guilty, and an estimated 2,800 to 2,900 people were sentenced to death. Sixty-two percent of the people appearing before this court received the death sentence; the rest were imprisoned in Auschwitz, which usually meant death. The youngest sentenced was fifteen, the oldest eighty. The fifteen-year-old, a girl, was sentenced to death for allegedly stealing a doll from a German child.

In 1947, U.S. authorities refused a Polish extradition request for Thummler. Interest in him was revived in the sixties, when he appeared as a witness in a war-crimes trial. An indictment was made in 1969, but a West German court ruled that, in his capacity as a judge, he had been acting within the law at the time, and so it refused to take further action. The appeal was likewise rejected, on the ground that the witness's testimony was of doubtful veracity—due to the terrible events and suffering he had endured! In 1979, a prosecutor in Stuttgart again suspended action against Thummler, at the same time stating that a possible murder charge had gone past the time set by the statute of limitations. Thummler has never stood in front of a court to answer for his crimes.[32]

"KEMPA"

Another important underground figure who perished at the hands of Johannes Thummler was Konstanty Kempa. Kempa was born on February 27, 1916, in the Silesian town of Labedy, near Gleiwitz (now Gliwice), into a family with a rich patriotic tradition. From 1931 to 1935 he attended the Cadet School in Lwów, probably motivated by the family's tradition of taking part in national uprisings.

When the war broke out, he immediately distinguished himself in the battle of Korczynek, where he destroyed nine Nazi tanks with a crew of only seven men and one piece of antitank artillery. He was forced to surrender, but later escaped and joined the underground.

Although it is difficult to establish all the underground connections he had, it is known that he fought with the soldier-poet Waclaw Stacherski, taking part in acquiring and storing weapons, sabotage operations and propaganda actions. His fiancée, Lucja, two sisters and a brother also took part in underground activities. He and Lucja married on June 21, 1942, and a son was born a year later. Secret meetings often took place in their home, and on more than one occasion Lucja used the baby carriage to smuggle weapons.

In time, Kempa was appointed inspector in the Department of Press and Information of the Home Army, and assigned to gather information on the concentration camp at Auschwitz, while also organizing "drops" of food and medicine to the camp. He lived in the town of Auschwitz with the Dylik family and was employed at a German gravel firm, a position that allowed him relatively free movement in the area around the camp.

Kempa's network of informants extended throughout northern Silesia. In Auschwitz itself, one of the most valued sources of information was an SS man who worked in an administrative office, and whose identity has never been established. He is known only by the pseudonym with which he occasionally signed his reports: "Karol." At one point, he let Kempa know that he was informing on the Nazis because of his conscience, out of a feeling that he had a moral obligation to let the world know what was going on at Auschwitz. His reports were apparently startling in their attention to the most scrupulous details concerning executions, the transport of prisoners and the involvement of the perpetrators on every level.

Among the prisoners, one of Kempa's best informants was "capo Jakub," probably Jakub Kozielczuk, the cellkeeper described in detail earlier in this book. Also working for Kempa were two Slovakian Jewish women, one of whom used the name Ili.

Kempa's Auschwitz network continued to function, despite the incredible pressures, until February 28, 1944; on that day, he was arrested at work, and a pistol and some documents concerning Auschwitz were found in his possession. On March 20, more conspirators were arrested, including Waclaw Stacherski, who was executed on September 18.

Kempa was "tried" on January 5, 1945, at the last sitting of the summary court headed by Johannes Thummler—the same court that sentenced Antoni Szlachcic—along with Mikolaj Kotowicz and Wladyslaw Saternus, all of whom had worked to acquire information on Auschwitz. Kempa was hung and the others shot on the same day.

Two years later, a former concentration-camp prisoner arrived at the home of Kempa's family with a note from him that the man had smuggled out in the heel of his shoe. The note read:

"Kempa" and Other
Names
Block 11, Cell 19 door
Main Camp
H: 12 inches

My dear family:

I have just been sentenced and in a few hours or even minutes they will kill me. Please, do not despair. I am giving my life for my country. God has given me good last moments, for I am spiritually strong. I received Holy Communion on New Year's Day and so go to my death united with God. Please pray for me a lot. Mother, take care of and raise my little Krysia and Stasiek until my beloved Lucja returns [his wife, Lucja, survived the war in a prison in Myslowice]. Live happily with everyone remaining. Farewell in God to you also, my dear in-laws, relatives; farewell children, my little orphans. Farewell Bolek and Stefan, my brother and sister-in-law. My dearest Lucja! To the end of my life I think of you, for you are my one alone. I love you all. Farewell. Be with God. My spirit will always be with you and the children. Live with God. I have a strong faith in God and the Holy Virgin. Farewell in God.

Husband, father, son, brother, son-in-law, brother-in-law,

Kostek[33]

"FOR POLAND, TO THE OVEN"

One of the people in Block 11 sentenced to death by Thummler managed to pen this laconic inscription onto one of the beams above the three-tiered bunks where prisoners slept. Most tourists miss these inscriptions because they are on the ceiling over their heads.

"He goes in the path of his father, for Poland, to the oven"
Golinski, Bronistow
born January 7, 1925, in Cieszyn
Block 11, ground floor
Main Camp
H: 2.5 inches
W: 5 inches

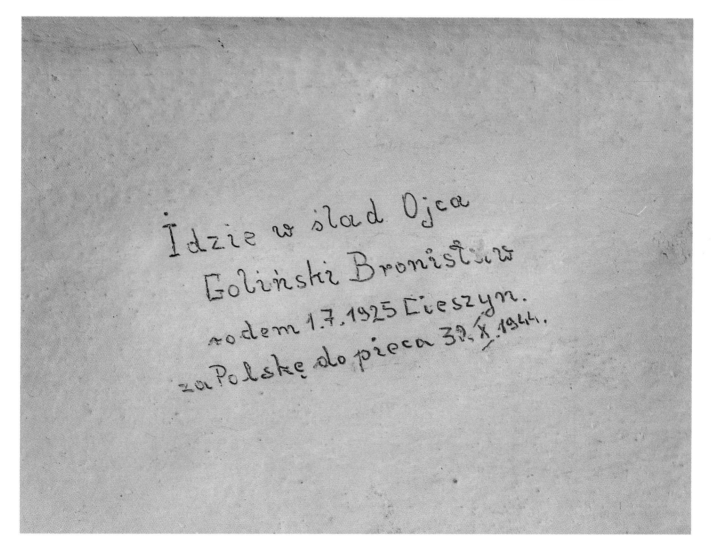

"16 YEARS OLD"

Zofia Zdrowak was only sixteen years old on December 3, 1944, when a band of partisans, four Auschwitz escapees, came down from the mountains with a plan to help the wife of one of the Home Army leaders escape from the camp. Zofia was putting the finishing touches on an SS uniform that was to be used in the attempt.

At that moment an SS man, a Yugoslavian named Alex, who had been trying to gain their confidence, drove up on his bike and told them he would like to join the partisans. They balked at this, but he said he would be back in a short while with some weapons for them.

In about an hour and a half, a truckful of SS men drove up to the house, surrounded it and started firing. Zofia tossed a cache of grenades hidden in the attic down to the partisans fighting off the SS. But the odds were too great, and three of the partisans were killed. The fourth, captured, later managed to escape by jumping out of the vehicle taking him to the camp. The SS held their fire as Zofia ran out the back door to the neighbors, but she was soon captured, along with her mother, father and sister.

First she was held in cell 1 of Block 11, where she left her name inscribed on the wall, and later in cell 3. The Nazis questioned and beat her continuously for four days, until her back was black from the beatings, and her mother could recognize her only by the clothes she was wearing.

Since the interrogators were rotated, she finally got an SS man who did not beat her; he said he had a daughter her age. The Germans, seeing they would not get anything out of her, ended the questioning.

Zofia, her mother and sister were evacuated from Auschwitz on January 17, 1945, and managed to escape from the SS column in charge of them and hide until the end of the war.[34]

*"Zofia Zdrowak—16
Years Old"*
Block 11, Cell 1, wall
Main Camp
H: 3 inches
W: 3 inches

MARKING TIME

Keeping track of time is a way of keeping one's sanity, one's dignity and one's sense of connectedness to the world. In the camp at large, the daily rhythms of life, however distorted, nevertheless provided a sense of time and order.

In solitary confinement, however, a person has to struggle to hold onto the consciousness of the cycles that mark life. The making of even a simple calendar can be an act of paramount importance.

All the calendars presented here were found in the basement cells of Block 11. Some cells were occupied by only one person at a time; others were packed to near suffocation. In all cases the prisoners were totally cut off from the rest of the camp.

The calendars range from carefully executed grids with the days of the week and the months painstakingly drawn, to simple columns of a few dots or slashes with no indication of the week, month or year. One calendar carved into the plaster wall of a cell is a kite with days marked off on the tail. Very often the last crossed-off date on a calendar indicates the day a prisoner was either released or executed.

CLOCK WITHOUT HANDS

This clock may have had some sort of movable indicators pivoting about the center. There are also several small, less legible clocks in the cells of Block 11.

Clock without Hands
Block 2
Birkenau
H: 24 inches

CALENDAR BY CELL WINDOW

This calendar, seen at the edge of the wall near the window, represents one of the simplest types of calendar, a vertical column of the numbered days of a given month. Even simpler than this are the calendars on which only dots or ticks are used to count off the days, which are not named.

Calendar by
Cell Window
Block 11, Cell 26
Main Camp
H: 12 inches

137

CALENDAR, AUGUST–DECEMBER 1944

This is perhaps the most common type of calendar found in Auschwitz—a simply drawn but accurate calendar that keeps track of the number of each day of the week. Many of them have, unfortunately, been gouged or destroyed by early tourists to the camp museum. Most are in cells that are not accessible to tourists.

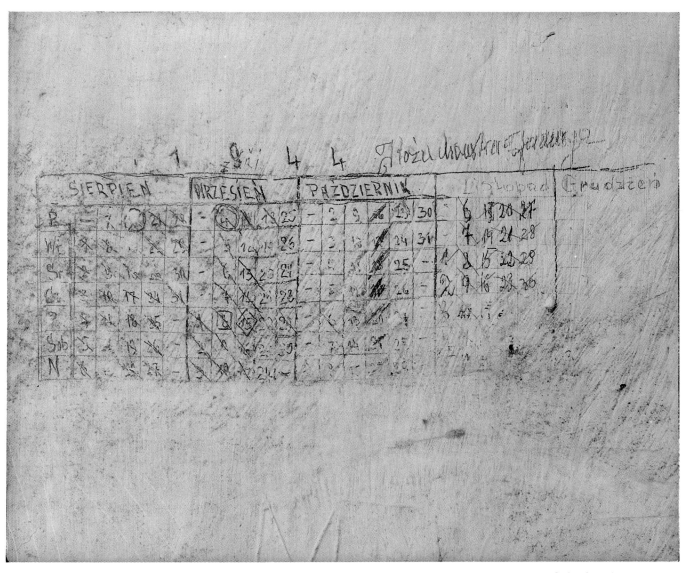

Calendar, August–
December 1944
Block 11, Cell 24
Main Camp
H: 4 inches
W: 10 inches

139

CALENDAR IN
POLISH AND GERMAN

Interesting here is the precision with which most of the numbers were drawn. The use of Polish and German words together is not unusual, because German was at one point the main second language in Poland. In the concentration camps, of course, it was the primary language.

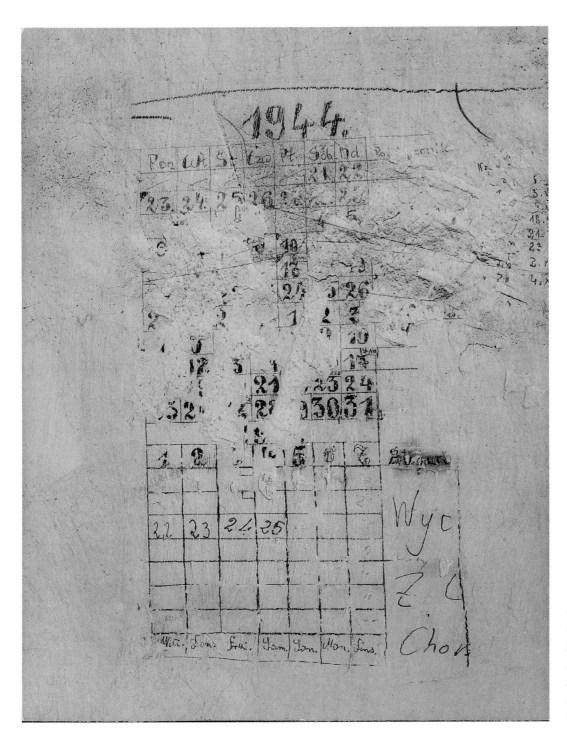

Calendar in Polish and German, October–December 1944
Block 11, Cell 24
Main Camp
H: 16.5 inches
W: 12 inches

"GOD HELP" CALENDAR

The second word is misspelled, and the calendar is divided into three ten-day weeks, leading to the conclusion that its maker was semiliterate. He was the same Kajzer Max who made the drawing of the town of Auschwitz and the autobiographical landscape shown earlier, and the calendar and drawings are in the same cell. The month is August, but, because of the way the weeks are shown, it is impossible to determine the year.

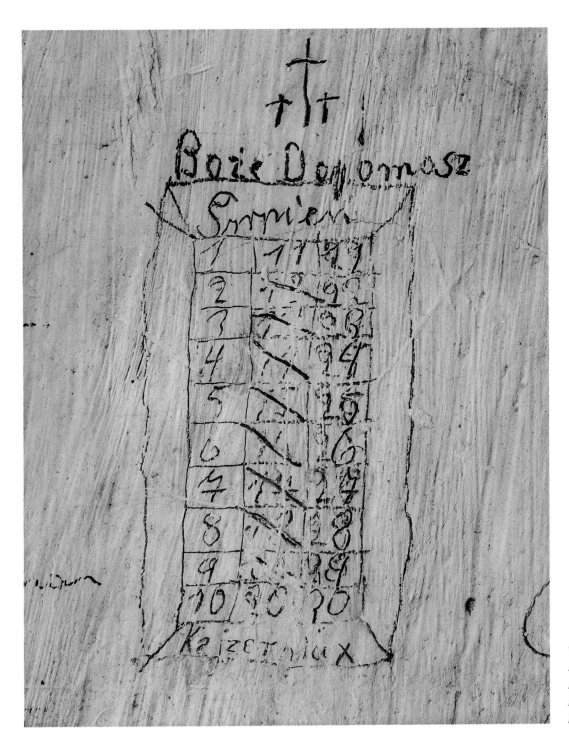

"God Help" Calendar,
signed Kajzer Max
Block 11, Cell 26
Main Camp
H: 4 inches

143

CALENDAR WITH CLASSICAL HEAD AND RUSSIAN INSCRIPTION

There is a small, incomplete calendar in the top left of the frame and a small heart just beneath it. The inscription indicates that the Russian who wrote it was being punished for an escape attempt.

*Calendar with Classical
Head and Russian
Inscription:
"Maksimovich was
imprisoned here for
escaping"
Block 11, Cell 11
Main Camp
H: 5.5 inches*

145

CALENDAR AND SCRATCHED-OUT POEM

Many of the calendars and inscriptions on the walls of the basement cells of Block 11 were unfortunately gouged away, as can be seen here. There are two possible explanations for this. One is that they were defaced by the SS. Former Block 11 record-keeper Jan Pilecki told me that this is unlikely, however, since the SS men rarely went into the cells.

The more likely explanation is that the damage was done in the period between 1948 and 1950 when Auschwitz was open to visitors but not yet organized as a museum. Many Poles who were inmates during the war came back to have another look at the place where they were incarcerated. Some of them simply left their names and hometowns scribbled on the walls, along with the date of their visit. Judging by the way in which the inscriptions were gouged, most of the serious damage may have been done by one person. Sometime early in the 1950s the cells were closed to tourists; only one or two can now be seen, and those only through barred doors. The others are seen occasionally by a few of the museum staff, including Adam Cyra, who are interested in tracing the stories behind the images.

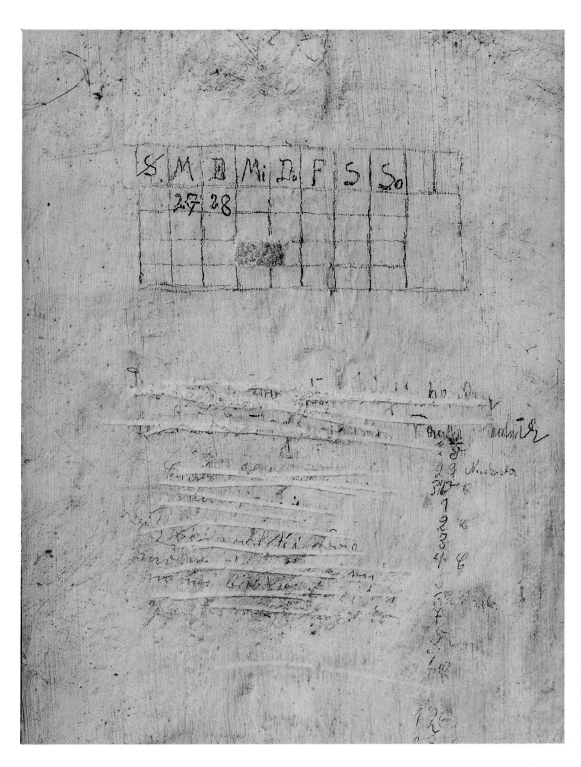

Calendar and
Scratched-out Poem
Block 11, Cell 6
Main Camp
H: 11 inches

STEFAN JASIENSKI'S CALENDAR

For Jasienski's story, see "The Commando," in the chapter "Heroes." This calendar, on the doorjamb of the cell where he was kept, is the only clue to the date of his death; it seems likely that he was executed shortly after the calendar's last date.

Stefan Jasienski's
Calendar
Block 11,
Cell 21,
doorjamb
Main Camp
H: 2.5 inches

KITE CALENDAR

The notion of time floating away on a kite is at the same time curiously whimsical and tragic. To the right of the kite are traces of a drawing of a female nude, most of which have been scratched away. In the upper left is a circle with crosshatching, which may also be a calendar.

150

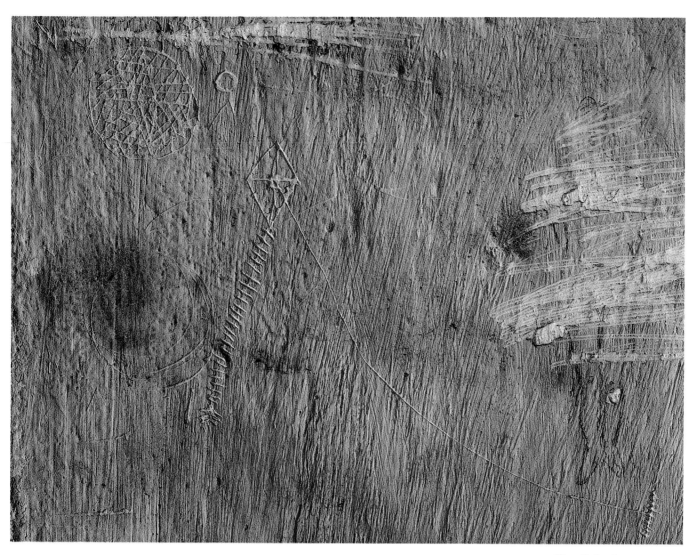

Kite Calendar
Block 11, Cell 3
Main Camp
H: 13 inches

CALENDAR WITH INSCRIPTION "THE END"

"The end" here probably refers to the maker's impending execution, since this was a common fate for prisoners in the bunker. Yet it could also mean the end of a punishment sentence, since prisoners from the camp were often punished for minor infractions, such as smoking, with a term of several days or weeks in the bunker.

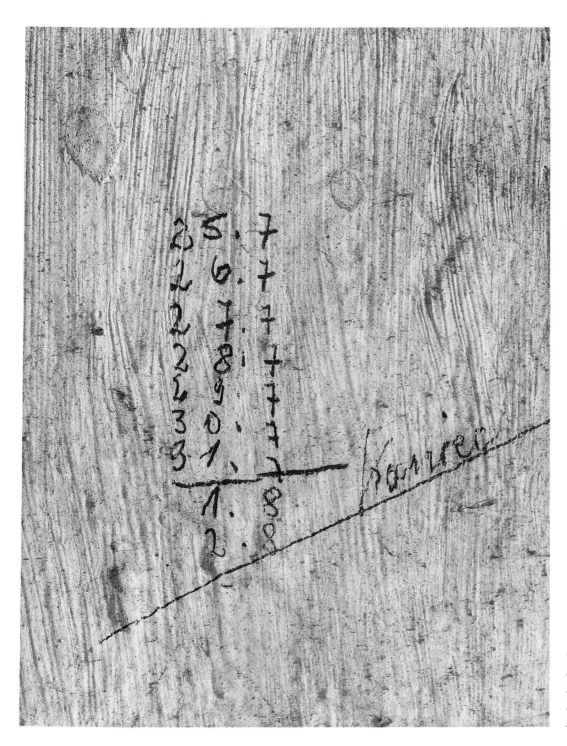

Calendar with
Inscription "The End"
Block 11, Cell 6
Main Camp
H: 2.5 inches

EPITAPHS

The most numerous category of markings found at Auschwitz is that of simple names and numbers left by prisoners who seem to have been concerned only with noting their own passing. In one of the most basic affirmative acts, a man leaves his name, by way of saying nothing more than "I am."

In some cases they left names with no numbers; in others, numbers with no names. Sometimes there are both, along with a hometown and date of birth; sometimes there are just initials. The names are Jewish, Russian, German, Dutch, Hungarian, Yugo-slavian, Greek, French, Italian, and, most frequently, Polish.

A letter inside an inverted triangle indicated the first letter of a prisoner's nationality; thus, a Pole had to wear on his camp uniform a triangle enclosing the letter *P*. For a Jew, a second triangle was inverted over the first one to form a Star of David, and many prisoners identified themselves as Jews by leaving behind this mark, or as Polish Jews by putting a *P* inside the star, even though the latter combination was not part of the official marking system.[35] This symbol is often found scratched alongside a prisoner's name or number.

Many prisoners who left their marks behind did so in several places in one cell, or, when they were moved around, in several cells. Leaving one's name on a brick was a way of retaining some sense of identity, and perhaps gave a shred of satisfaction in the knowledge that one's passing would somehow be noted.

Why prisoners often identified themselves by their prison numbers only is hard to say. It seems to be a sign of submission, but perhaps it shows simply an acceptance of the reality that they were now more number than name. Despite the precision of German recordkeeping, it is not unusual to find several prisoners' names listed under one number. This, plus the fact that many of the records were destroyed, makes it often impossible to trace a prisoner's identity by the number alone.

NAMES CARVED IN BRICKS

These inscriptions are located on the back of a building that seems to have been a bathhouse. The place must have been out of the direct view of guards and watchtowers, because the prisoners would have needed a fair amount of unsupervised time to carve their names here. These are three of a series of about ten that were found in this area, made mostly by Jewish women prisoners. There are also a few inscriptions in Russian and some Russian stars on the same wall.

"Mirjam Braun," Carved in Brick
Bathhouse, Women's Camp
Birkenau

"Marta Goldstein," Carved in Brick
Bathhouse, Women's Camp
Birkenau

"Lucja Gold, Lodz," Carved in Brick Bathhouse, Women's Camp Birkenau

HUNGARIAN NAMES CARVED IN BRICK

For some reason, there were several Hungarian inscriptions on the same wall, within a few feet of each other. The two shown here indicate where their makers were from: Debrecen, in eastern Hungary, and Nagyvaradi, a part of Hungary before the war, but now part of Romania. The inscription "Nagyvaradi Getto bol" means "from the Nagyvaradi ghetto," indicating that the author was Jewish. There are three Zoltan Wiesels listed in the German camp records, all of them Jews from Hungary, and three Laszlo Nagys, also Hungarian Jews. Nothing more is known about them.

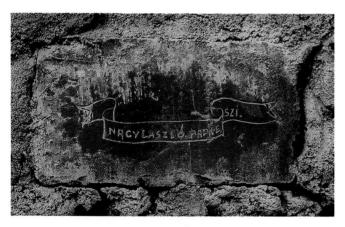

*"Nagy Laszlo Papkeszi,"
on Banner Carved in
Brick
Exterior of Block 7
Main Camp*

*"Zoltan Wiesel" and
"Nagyvaradi Ghetto,"
Inscribed in Brick
Exterior of Block 7
Main Camp*

STAR OF DAVID AND NUMBER CARVED IN BRICK

The number 130234 appears in camp records as belonging to Jan Wiater, brought to Auschwitz from Krakow on July 17, 1943. The Star of David means he was Jewish. There is a record in the museum archives that a package sent to him in the camp was returned to the sender, which means that he either had perished or had been sent to another camp. The star and number can be seen on the outside of the building at eye level.

"WOLF ZELMANOWICZ," CARVED IN BRICK

The name and native town of this prisoner indicate that he came from a part of Poland that was under the Prussian Partition prior to 1918.

"AUSCHWITZ," CARVED IN BRICK

This is the only known example of the name Auschwitz occurring on the walls of the camp. The grid pattern next to it may have been used as a crude map of the camp.

Star of David and Number, Carved in Brick Exterior of Block 9 Main Camp

"Wolf Zelmanowicz," Carved in Brick Exterior of Block 9 Main Camp

"Auschwitz," Carved in Brick Induction Center Birkenau

NAMES AND NUMBERS
ON CELL DOOR

This was the most densely inscribed cell door in the basement of Block 11, but there are others nearly as crowded. On this door, the names are mostly Polish; a few are Russian. Several names and numbers appear in more than one place on the door.

There is a noticeable darkening around the peephole in the door. This was caused by oil from the skin that soaked into the wood when prisoners looked through the hole. Most did this with their right eye, which led to the rest of the face being pressed to the top and left of the hole. The oil and sweat on the faces of thousands of prisoners eventually created this visible mark on the wood.

Some of the numbers here can be traced through the incomplete camp records. Number 25404, for instance, belonged to Mieczyslaw Kulikowski, a camp surveyor who was hanged in a public execution of twelve resistance members on July 19, 1943.

NAMES AND NUMBERS
CARVED IN WELL

This photograph is actually upside down. The members of a well-digging kommando in the uncompleted Mexico sector of Birkenau had one of their group lean down into a still-wet cement pipe to leave this record of their existence. The well is located on what is now a private farm.

160

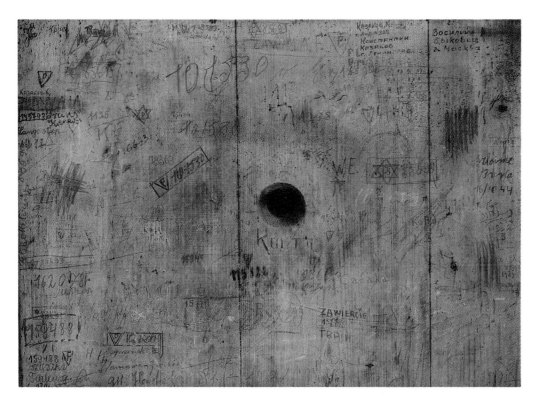

*Names and Numbers on
Cell Door
Block 11, Cell 16
Main Camp
H: 15 inches
W: 23 inches*

*Names and Numbers
Carved in Well
Birkenau, Mexico sector
H: 11 inches*

LAST WORDS

In view of the millions who passed through Auschwitz and the millions who died there, the handful of brief poems I found on the cell doors and walls of Block 11 seem pitifully few. Must these words represent the dying thoughts of so many? Did the millions of victims spend their final moments thinking about things people think about all their lives—God, love, fate and death?

Most of these poems require no comment. The farewell messages on the ceiling beams in Block 11 were written by prisoners just before their executions. The judge who condemned them to death is described earlier, under " 'Laura'—Antoni Szlachcic." The other inscriptions were found in the basement of Block 11, the so-called bunker, where prisoners usually knew that they were awaiting execution.

I end with Bernard Swierczyna's poem, which summarizes the essential nature of the conflict that was waged at Auschwitz: a war between the Nazis, who sought to degrade and ultimately obliterate their victims, and the prisoners, who struggled to hold onto their dignity and humanity.

"I only wanted to be a man
   Not a soul-less collection of numbers . . ."

Poem on Cell Wall
"Whoever in his life
has not known what
freedom is
Here will find it
and love it."
signed K.F.
Block 11, Cell 6
Main Camp
H: 2.5 inches
W: 4 inches

Mickiewicz
Paraphrase
on Cell Door
"Whoever has not
known bitterness
even once
Will never know
this sweetness."
From "Grandfather's
Eve" by the Polish
romantic poet
Adam Mickiewicz
Block 11, Cell 6
Main Camp
H: 3 inches
W: 6 inches

164

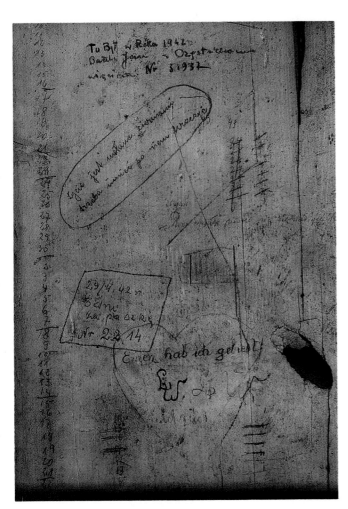

Poem and Inscriptions on Cell Wall
"Here in the year 1942
was Jan B . . . from
Czestochowa Prisoner No. 31937."

"Life is strewn with thorns;
One must know how to pass through it."

"I have loved only one man." [German]
Block 11, Cell 6
Main Camp
H: 9 inches   W: 13 inches

Poem on Cell Door
"Forget if you can, of my love;
Forget if you can, that you loved me."
Block 11, Cell 28
Main Camp
H: 7.5 inches

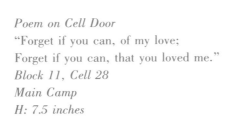

(Left): Farewell Poem Before Execution
"I have enough of this battle,
May I know peace,
May I perish in peace,
In this cruel war."
Jan. 6, 1945
Tondos Adam Jezor
Katowitzstr. 20
Block 11, ceiling beam on ground floor
Main Camp
H: 4 inches   W: 6 inches

(Above): Farewell Poem Before Execution
"I lived, Lord, because you wanted it,
I die because you ordained it;
Save me you can,
O Great God."
Post. Luczak Jozef
Block 11, ceiling beam on ground floor
Main Camp
H: 4 inches   W: 6 inches

(Left): Farewell Poem Before Execution
"In this last hour of my life,
I bid farewell to all of you remaining brothers.
For I am condemned to death.
Please do not forget about me after the war."
Main Camp
H: 6 inches   W: 6 inches

BERNARD SWIERCZYNA ("BENEK")

The final picture in this book is of a cell-door poem by a man who died in the last execution held in the Auschwitz men's camp, less than a month before the camp's liberation.

Bernard Swierczyna had just been married and was starting to study law when the war broke out. As a second lieutenant, he took part in the defense of Poland until further resistance was impossible, and then went back to civilian life. The Germans arrested him as a prisoner of war, but then released him (because he was a Silesian) on December 23, 1939.

Swierczyna went to Krakow to avoid being arrested again, but later tried to return to his home in Myslowice in order to be near his wife, who was due to give birth shortly. In order to cross the border into Silesia, he decided to seek help from a girl he had grown up with who now worked at the passport office in Gestapo headquarters. The woman not only refused, but also threatened him, saying that he would never return home. A few minutes after stepping out of Gestapo headquarters, he was arrested. On July 18, 1940, he arrived at Auschwitz, where he was given the number 1393.

In February of 1941 he joined the ZWZ, or Zwiazek Walki Zbrojnej (Union of Armed Struggle), one of the resistance groups in the camp. Many of the leaders of this group died in 1943, victims of a large Nazi action against the ZWZ. Swierczyna managed to evade their fate, and became the leader of the military arm of the Home Army resistance in the camp.

But his resistance activity was to end tragically the next year. Five members of the group planned an escape in a laundry truck driven by a bribed SS man. The German betrayed them, however, and instead of being driven through the camp gates, they were taken to Block 11. Zbigniew Raynoch and Czeslaw Duzel immediately committed suicide with poison. Swierczyna, Piotr Piaty (see picture of his name earlier) and an Austrian named Ernst Burger were imprisoned in the basement of Block 11, where they were soon joined by two other Austrian conspirators, Rudolf Frie-mel and Ludwig Vesely. At the same time, the Nazis carried out a raid on the town of Leki Zasole, shooting Konstanty Jagiello, an escaped inmate who had been waiting to take in the new escapees.

The men were executed on the gallows that stood in front of the camp kitchen after the evening roll call on December 30, 1944. They died crying out in Polish and German: "Down with Hitler! Down with fascism! Long live Poland!"[36]

Bernard Swierczyna's Cell-Door Poem,
Written Before His Execution
"I only wanted to be a man
Not a soul-less collection of numbers
To link my being with future ages
To know the code of future histories
Force took me by betrayal
And put me behind bars
But did not break my honor
Even the executioner cannot do that.
—How sweet it is to die for the fatherland."
Bernard Swierczyna, 27 December 1944
Block 11, Cell 28
Main Camp

NOTE ON THE PHOTOGRAPHY

The camera used on this project was an 18-×-24-cm. East German Mentor Panorama, which can sometimes be found in Warsaw camera shops for a reasonable price. The large-format camera was necessary in order to render faithfully the minute surface detail of the subjects. It also enabled me to make contact prints, thus eliminating the need for a large-format enlarger (which is hard to come by in this part of the world).

I used Kodak Plus X and Tri X film, which had to be specially cut down to the 18-×-24-cm. size. Development was usually N + 2 in Zone System terminology, but ranged from N to N + 3. HC-110 developer was used in concentrations ranging from normal to four times normal in order to keep the time down. In the case of the pencil drawings, the originals were of such low contrast that the contrast had to be boosted at every stage of the photographic process.

The negatives were printed in an ordinary contact-printing frame under an enlarger, onto Kodak Elite #3 paper. The prints were developed in Dektol diluted 1:2 and also in a strong hydroquinone developer (Beers 7), from 2 to 5 minutes. The only manipulations applied at this stage were to even out brightness differences caused by uneven lighting. The prints were selenium toned at a dilution of 1:30 for six minutes.

Most of the subjects were lighted by two 1000-watt quartz lights, sometimes bounced off umbrellas, sometimes through the umbrellas, sometimes directly, and occasionally obliquely. The diffused light used in most of the photographs in fact closely reproduced the quality of the light in which the originals are seen. Exposures ranged from several seconds to 20 minutes. Due to the size and weight of the camera, I had to work with an assistant, because it was often impossible simultaneously to set the camera's movements and to tighten the setscrews on the tripod. The most difficult shots were those where we had no electrical outlets available. Some of these shots took several hours to set up, and even focusing was a chore. The subjects had to be lighted by an electronic flash that was "popped" up to 30 times to "paint" the subject in enough light for an exposure.

For several of the photographs, we had to build scaffolds for the camera under the ceiling beams where certain inscriptions were located. At the other extreme, it was sometimes necessary to mount the camera just above the floor in order to get the necessary distance from the subject; in such situations, I had to lie on my back to see through the lens. And in some instances, special electric lines had to be threaded up several floors to light the paintings.

Toward the end of the project, my assistant was drafted into the Polish army. Since working alone with the large-format camera had proved unfeasible, I then used my father's Rolleiflex SL66 with the new Kodak T-Max 100 film, at double the recommended speed and developed in a double-strength solution of the T-Max developer. Ilford Multigrade fiber-based paper, used with the higher-number filters, further increased the contrast. The results proved comparable to the contact prints, and only under high magnification can a difference be detected.

NOTES

1. Jozef Szajna, in *The Art of the Holocaust* by Janet Blatter and Sybil Milton. London: Pan Books, 1981.

2. The estimate of the number of people killed at Auschwitz ranges between one and four million. The Russian commission set up to investigate war crimes immediately after the war came up with a figure of four million. This figure, which in fact is still quoted in guidebooks to the State Museum at Auschwitz, was based on information available at the time, including the testimony of camp commandant Rudolf Hoss and the theoretical capacity of the crematoria.

   Modern scholars, with more complete access to documents, have revised this figure downward, on the basis of a study of transport lists of people sent to Auschwitz from various countries. The figure they come up with is approximately 1.5 million, which includes the 300,000 of the 405,000 numbered prisoners who died.

   It is generally agreed that Jews made up about ninety percent of the victims at Auschwitz. The Jew had to carry not only the burden of his own individual suffering, but also the knowledge that it was his entire race that the Nazis were trying to exterminate.

   In all likelihood the Germans' policy of extermination, which had already been applied to Jews, gypsies and Soviet prisoners of war, would have been extended to the Poles and other Slavic peoples had the war gone on much longer.

3. Janina Jaworska, *Nie Wszystek Umre*. Warsaw: Ksiazka i Wiedza, 1975, p. 102.

4. This text in German reads:

   Der mensch zieht sein Los bei der Geburt und muss den Weg gehen, der ihm vorbestimmt ist ob er will oder nicht. Das Schicksal ist ohne Mitgefuhl ohne Liebe und fragt keinen, wie es ihm recht ist. So laufen die Wege ins Ungewisse, gerade und krumm, bergauf und bergab, schmal und breit. Mancher stolpert und fallt, steht wieder auf, wirft sich den Staub, die . . . ab, die Schramme heilt schnell und alles ist wieder gut. Vielen winkt ein schones Ziel, wo die Sonne scheint und das Gluck wartet und das grosse Licht uberstrahlt ihren Weg, damit sie sicher gehen. Aber da sindauch Strassen, die ins Dunkel fuhren und an Abgrunden dahin, auf denen Gefahr und Tod lauern und wer sich auf ihm befindet [?] fur den erlischt die Sonne. Immer freilich sind fur . . . die Gnade und das Wunder [?] unterwegs, nur sind sie schwer zu sehen und zu begreifen, fur die, die im Dunkeln wandern mussen.

5. Jozef Kret, "Dzien w Karnej Kompanii," *Zeszyty Oswiecimskie*, 1957, 1:147–180.

6. Teresa Ceglowska, "Karne Kompanie w KL Auschwitz," *Zeszyty Oswiecimskie* 17:155–198.

7. Archives of the State Museum at Auschwitz (hereafter ASMA).

8. Wojciech Kielar, *Anus Mundi*. Krakow: Wydawnictwo Literackie, 1980.

9. Jerzy Debski, "Camp Signs of KL Auschwitz in the Collection of the State Museum at Auschwitz," unpublished manuscript, ASMA.

10. Maria Slisz, *Oswiadczenie* 88:198, ASMA.

11. M. Koscielniak, *Bilder von Auschwitz*, Frankfurt, 1982.

12. Primo Levi, *Se questo e un uomo*. Turin: Giuli Einaudi, 1958, pp. 36–37.

13. ASMA.

14. Eulalia Kurdej, *Oswiadczenie* 66:134–136, ASMA.

15. Janet Blatter and Sybil Milton, *op. cit.*

16. *Xawery Dunikowski i Polscy Artysci w Obozach Koncentracyjnych*, catalog to the exhibit "Xawery Dunikowski and Polish Artists in Concentration Camps," at the National Museum, Warsaw, 1985.

17. Irena Stefanska, "Medycyna w oswiecimskiej plastyce obozowej," *Przeglad Lekarski*, 1977, 1:111.

18. ASMA.

19. Kielar, *op. cit.*; Adam Cyra, "Milosc w Piekle," *Panorama*, Warsaw, 1986, 7:20–21.

20. Erich Kulka, *Escape from Auschwitz*. South Hadley, MA: Begin and Garvey, 1986, especially pp. 131–134.

21. Since Pestek arrived at Auschwitz at the end of May, this would put the time of his death around the end of June. German army records, however, give the date of his execution as October 8, 1944, which may explain the later dates seen by his signature on the door of Cell 26. See Death Certificate No. 15195/1948, Stamdesamtes I, West Berlin.

22. Sidra DeKoven Ezrahi, *The Holocaust in Literature*.

23. Jozef Otowski, *Wspomnienie* 103:57–59, ASMA.

24. Levi, *op. cit.*

25. Tadeusz Sobolewicz, *Wytrzymalem Wiec Jestem*. Katowice: "Slask," 1986, pp. 114–115.

26. Zdzislaw Ryn and Stanislaw Klodzinski, "Patologia sportu w obozach koncentracyjnych," *Przeglad Lekarski*, 1974, 31:51–55.

27. The book, *Boxer i Smierc* (The Boxer and Death), by Jozef Hen, was the basis for a film with the same title made in Bratislava in 1962 by Peter Solan.

28. Since the exact circumstances of his death have never come to light, it is impossible to exclude completely the possibility that he was liquidated by the resistance as a preventive measure.

29. Adam Cyra, "Niewyjasnione Okolicnosci Smierci Urbana," *Kierunki*, 6, Feb. 9, 1986; "Zyciorys z celi smierci," *Panorama*, 1985, 15:12–13.

30. Adam Cyra, "Spadochron, Colt, i KL Auschwitz," *Tygodnik Polski*, 1987, 223:8–9.

31. Adam Cyra, "Kat i Ofiara," *Oswiecimski Chemik*, 1987, 576:2.

32. Jozef Musiol, *Sedzia i kat, jeden dzien doktora Thummlera*. Warsaw: MON, 1986.

33. Zbyszko Bednorz, *Lata krecie i orlowe*, Warsaw: PAX, 1987, pp. 68–92.

34. Zofia Zdrowak, conversation with author; Anna Zdrowak, *Oswiadczenie* 42:31–32, ASMA.

35. Tadeusz Iwaszko, in *Auschwitz, Nazi Extermination Camp*. Warsaw: Interpress, 1985, pp. 56–62.

36. Adam Cyra, "Benek," *Katolik*, Jan. 19, 1986, p. 13.